GW00787948

Bygones be Bygones

ABOUT THE AUTHOR

David Hill likes to say that he was born in Norwich early in the last century, *went* to Town Close House School and Epsom College, but was *educated* in the army. He has lived in many places in Norfolk and Suffolk and has now settled near Diss.
Bygones be Bygones is the last of his trilogy of books, each offering a light-hearted account of his involvement in the world of antiques and bygones, working with his son, William.

Bygones be Bygones

David Hill

Drawings by Fenella Noble

Larks Press

Published by the Larks Press

Ordnance Farmhouse, Guist Bottom
Dereham, Norfolk NR20 5PF
01328 829207
Larks.Press@btinternet.com
www.booksatlarkspress.co.uk

Printed by the Lanceni Press
Garrood Drive, Fakenham
01328 851578
October 2005

Also by David Hill

A Living in the Past

A Good Deal

No part of this book or its illustrations may be reproduced in any form
without the permission of the publishers and author.

British Library Cataloguing-in-Publication Data
A catalogue record for this book is available
from the British Library.

© David Hill 2005

ISBN 1 904006 28 0

LOT 1
Looking back over my shoulder

'Do you know what you are going to say this afternoon ?' enquired Mary.

'Yes, I think so,' I replied, rather guiltily, because I had been invited at least three months earlier to present the prizes. I had been thinking about it from time to time but as always when an event is far enough in the future it is easy to put off serious consideration. Now time had almost run out.

'I suppose,' I said, 'that there are three things to be mentioned. First, my thanks for being invited to the Fiftieth Anniversary occasion. Second, to say something about the achievements of those fifty years, and then to round off with something amusing or even memorable.'

'Well, try not to be a bore and don't go on too long,' she advised. As she is an ex-schoolmistress and we had by then been married forty years she did know what she was talking about.

I remembered it all this month as I set off for the Seventieth Anniversary celebration at the same school.

William took me to the party. He is also an old boy of the school and, rather to my surprise, clocked up his own half-century this month. We've come a long way together and, as I recall, we have never been in conflict. In fact, if Richmal Crompton hadn't got there first, this trilogy could well have been entitled *Just William*.

Right from the beginning, when Mary and I proposed starting our antiques business at the Old Forge, William was involved. He came home to help, and without him I am not sure that we would ever have got started. There was a lot of hard work to be done setting up our workshop, making the old forge presentable, assembling stock and putting in place the organisation of the business. There were also a lot of laughs and some strange experiences, some of which I recorded in *A Living in the Past*.

One of our first visitors when we moved into the blacksmith's cottage was a friend whom we had not seen for a number of years. She got out of her car, took one look and said, 'This must be a dream come true'. She was absolutely right. Our thatched cottage, in its own half-acre with mature fruit trees, embodied most of the elements of a townswoman's dream of a place in the country, 'far from the madding crowd'. I should perhaps mention that it also concealed behind its smiling welcome many of her most-feared features, such things as vermin in the roof, erratic public services and trouble with drains. None of these were new to us. The novelty of our new home was the swift-flowing stream forming part of the boundary of the property. It was this which had captured our hearts.

You could say that at this stage William played the role of supporting character. We ourselves often felt that we were acting in a play and learning our words as we went along. Later William joined the business full time, and when Mary and I decided (or, to be more accurate, when Mary decided) that it was time for us to retire, he took charge and moved to the Swan. Rehabilitating a fairly typical old Norfolk pub to create a family home, a place of work and an antiques shop was a daunting task. We opened on schedule though it would be untrue to say that we were really ready to do so. Even before the signwriter had finished his work, faithful friends and customers had found us. Again it was rather like being on stage with the scenery still being erected while noises off were provided by concrete-mixer and hammers. The house lights were not yet working, but we were back in business.

The next few years, of which I wrote in *A Good Deal*, were followed by the sale of the Swan, and William, with his growing family, moved to Ford Farm. He no longer had a shop, trading instead through antiques centres, working the salerooms and buying in over an ever enlarging catchment area. Our roles were now clearly reversed. I had definitely become the supporting character and almost succeeded in retiring.

Antiques, bygones and furniture restoration are still the main thrust of his business, but life on his smallholding has never lacked variety. My weekly visit may well start with bottle-feeding lambs, proceed through a visit to a farm sale or saleroom before getting to the workshop and more routine activities. In addition to William's family other minor characters enter the plot – Russell the ram, Boris the Muscovy duck and Half-wit Harry the dog all have walk-on parts.

So now we come to *Bygones be Bygones*, with greater attention paid to the items passing through our hands, and activities in the workshop, which is the heart of the business. We still see a delightful slice of life through the workshop windows. The stream and willow trees at the Old Forge, the common and the windmill at the Swan are replaced by views over the ever-changing fields and down to the alder carrs beyond Swangey Lakes. There is no lack of wildlife, and no lack of good laughs, yet we still get through a good deal of work.

Bygones be Bygones completes the trilogy. I hope that I haven't gone on too long and been a bore!

LOT 2
'I remember, I remember...'

My birth certificate indicates that I was born in West Wymer, which has a pleasantly rural sound, or maybe trans-Atlantic. It was in fact a district of Norwich, and the happy event took place at No 11, Grove Avenue. No, I don't remember the house where I was born because the family moved when I was one year old. I also have to believe that I was christened in the 'Tin Tabernacle' at the top end of the avenue.

I do remember the Fountain which stood at the junction of the Newmarket and Ipswich roads. When it was removed, the statue which formed its centrepiece was placed in the garden of the Norfolk and Norwich Hospital, just a few yards away.

All these things came to my mind this morning when I walked into the workshop and saw two wooden boxes emblazoned 'Colman's Mustard'. They also reminded me of the fact that although various members of my family have crept into these notes, I have made only passing reference to my father.

Almost exactly a hundred years ago, Father joined J. and J. Colman Ltd of Norwich, and no, he had nothing to do with mustard except indirectly. He spent the whole of his working life with the firm, in the course of which he became responsible for the Blue Mills, Sawmills, Box-making department, Lemon Barley crystals and timber-buying in Germany and Scandinavia. As a sideline in World War 2 he was 'O/C Junk', which seems to have meant that he was responsible for a fair range of improvisation and much make-do-and-mend.

In later years he also became a director of James Southall and Co. Ltd. Now there's a couple of names to juggle with, Colman's Mustard and Start-Rite shoes – they sound like items from those old-style geography books from which one was required to learn the chief manufactured products from all the main population centres. Those two firms did indeed epitomise the resurgence of industrial growth in Norwich following the decline in the weaving industry.

A charming picture of the early days of the Colman enterprise was given by Mrs John Willis, which I reproduce from the *Financial Times* of January 1925, the year of her death.

'Perhaps I should add a touch of romance to what you have said about Colman's, for my memory reaches back to the early beginnings when a one-armed man did the whole of the firm's packing , and as a tiny girl I would help him on busy days to fix labels. I can still picture my father, Jeremiah Colman, in the counting room at the old watermill at Stoke, with bowls in which the latter would personally mix and sample the admixture of seeds.

That mustard was made seems to have originated merely from the suggestion of a caller on the former owner of the mill, for on its transfer to Jeremiah Colman there figured in the purchase agreement an item of fifteen pounds two shillings for mustard seed. With its sale began the association of Colman and mustard.'

My personal addition to that story is that the last time I saw Stoke Mill Mary and I were attending a wedding reception; a new use for an old building. It is now a well-appointed restaurant in a delightful setting. My old friend Mr Morse, a former miller at Saxlingham Mill, just up the river, would have been amazed by such a transformation, especially the modern cloakroom facilities. At Saxlingham the wooden 'throne' was mounted precariously up three rickety steps directly over the water-wheel.

I believe that my father enjoyed his work, especially while Colmans remained a private company, rather less after it went public and the strong family element became diluted. He certainly enjoyed his sport. This featured a partnership with his brother Leonard and their successes in the C.E.Y.M.S football team. He was a cricketer of some note, a reliable player on the tennis court and achieved a low handicap at golf, playing mainly at Eaton. The municipal course at Earlham came and went in a very short space of time. I saw the opening round played between Cotton and Havers where the University of East Anglia now stands. Those upper reaches of the Yare were my childhood playground.

Occasionally during school holidays I was allowed to visit father at Carrow works. I loved those visits. Food-packaging machinery, automatic weighing of the product, filling, sealing and labelling and the various forms of conveyors never failed to enchant me. The Blue Mill (destroyed in the Blitz) was an industrial version of the blue grottoes which one finds in tourist spots all round the Mediterranean. The whole building vibrated with grinding and mixing machinery and everything was lightly dusted with ultramarine blue. Father's office in the building was a noisy place. It was a source of entertainment to us that when using the phone in the office he spoke quite gently, yet when using it at home he tended to shout! He had a theory, which I half understand, that one can more effectively speak under a noise than over it.

I saw Robinson's Lemon Barley crystals almost from the beginning. The plant producing what became an internationally known product was staggeringly simple, almost an improvisation, partitioned off in the corner on three floors of other departments. In the tall starch ovens I was chiefly interested in the ingenious arrangement of chutes which brought the large blocks of starch down to ground level for further processing. Of course the

4

milling and packing of mustard in all its various forms and variety of containers was always at the heart of a visit.

At the far end of the Works, down by the river, was the Deal Ground, where timber was stacked alongside the sawmill where it was cut to requirement for box-making. The shriek of band saws ripping through timber is like no other, not necessarily a pleasant noise to all ears, but the fragrance of the fresh-cut timber can hardly fail to please even the most discerning.

Saw-milling is a dangerous occupation. One of Father's constant concerns was the safety of the machine operators, equalled only by the preoccupation with attempting to satisfy the Factory Inspector that everything possible was being done to that end. The story is told (and I've often told it myself) that on one occasion when he was becoming exasperated with the unreasonable demands of a particular inspector, he said, 'Miss Messiter, you can make a machine foolproof, but you can't make it bloody-foolproof'.

Even the printing works was full of fascination. Not everyone is introduced to lithography by an R.A. Only later did I come to appreciate the work of Mr Starling. Nor for that matter did I know that blue, starch, printing and wood were to feature largely in three of my later occupations.

The company's Annual Review lies on my desk as I write. I am happy to see that a Colman still heads the firm. The range of products also delights me, especially 'Cattlemen's Classic Sauce' in gallon containers, and a range of environmentally friendly household products. I am happy too to have a stake in the business for which, like so much more, I am indebted to my father.

Although we had a car by the time I was about sixteen Father never learned to drive. He continued to cycle to and from work each day. In earlier days he took me to school on the step of his bike. I've not seen such a thing in years and they are probably now illegal. I found my own way home on foot or, more excitingly, by being given a lift by George on his milk-cart. No bottles of milk in those days; George measured it out in pint or half-pint measures. In spite of that double journey with a day's work in between, Father was more often than not out in the garden for an hour or two after he got home. The garden was a large one and I don't remember that he had much help. Certainly I was not of much assistance – I suspect that few people are keen on gardening until they have one of their own.

There was one aspect of garden work in which I enthusiastically gave my help, ands that was in tree felling and planting. With Father I learned to use a double-handed crosscut saw, how to swing a felling axe, and even had a few goes with climbing irons. Father taught me all such useful things together with swimming, sailing, map-reading, campfire cookery and a whole host of others. What he didn't teach by instruction he taught by example, and I am happy to think that I absorbed much of his philosophy of life and standards of behaviour. He passed on his skills and enthusiasm for tennis to my sister, who lapped it all up to good effect. Being somewhat younger than she was, and a good deal less fiercely competitive, I was absolutely no use to her on the court, and I retired early from the unequal fray.

I am not painting much of a picture of my father, except that even thus far it is obvious that he fostered and shared our enthusiasms. We swam mostly at a charming spot in the river a little below Eaton Church. I see it as always sunny, the water crystal clear and the kingcups in the meadow as big as tulips! In fact that is how I see most of my childhood. There have been some grey and grim times since then, but it was a happy and secure base from which to embark on life's journey.

The last holiday I spent with Father was in the Lake District in 1937. Our departure from Euston was delayed while staff searched the train for IRA bombs. Some things don't change. I can best summarise the holiday by quoting from a picture postcard (postage one penny) which we sent to Mother.

> 'We had a wonderful day yesterday. We walked about twenty miles through Buttermere and by Crummock Water, through the Honister Pass and back along the river Derwent and the whole length of the lake. We both caught the sun. I am more stiff and sore than Daddy who *says* that he isn't stiff at all.
> Much love, David.'

That is how I like to remember him, fit, sunburnt and still able to outwalk me. The War was nearly on us, the second world war for his generation, and it took its toll. He lived to know his grandchildren but not long enough to enjoy a well-earned retirement.

LOT 3
Sheepfold

The note tacked to the workshop door read :

Plenty of jobs to be done in the workshop or come and help with sheep-dipping at Whitehall Farm.
Will

Apart from bottle-feeding lambs I've not had much to do with the sheep so, always ready to learn, I set off down the lane to the farm. On my way I thought about my old friend Jethro and a conversation we had recently.

'You don't know a lot about sheep', said Jethro. He was right. I had just exposed my ignorance by remarking that it was an odd thing that there was no distinctive breed of Norfolk sheep.

'That's where you are wrong, my friend. The Norfolk sheep is very distinctive indeed, it just happens that you don't see many of them nowadays…fact the only places you will see them will soon be in rare breed collections or perhaps at Whipsnade Zoo.'

In a monologue punctuated by sips from his pint of beer he went on to tell me that the original Norfolks were already becoming rare about two hundred years ago. They were well known for their hardiness, their good breeding characteristics and the fact that they were well suited to the rather wild and often sparse conditions in this area. Then, as the agricultural scene was changing towards arable farming, a more domesticated breed was needed. The Norfolk ram was crossed with Southdown ewes. The result for some strange reason became known as the Suffolk, and the rather wild athletic Norfolk with its large curled horns virtually disappeared.

I called for two more pints and in an attempt to even the score asked Jethro if he knew the story of the Throckmorton Jacket. 'Noo,' he said, 'Goo you on and tell me.' It so happened that Mary and I had recently returned from Worcester. While we were there we had done some brass-rubbing at Fladbury, including the Throckmorton brasses. These brasses are set up on altar tombs, which makes them much pleasanter to rub than the more usual scribble on a cold floor. Also, not having been trodden on by generations of feet, they are in excellent condition. It was there that we had unearthed the story about the jacket.

In 1811, as the result of a wager, a coat was made in Throckmorton from the wool off a sheep's back to the finished article, between sunrise and sunset. This triumph of 'manufacturing celerity', we were told, was witnessed by five thousand spectators who 'rent the air with acclamations!' The sheep were roasted whole on that same day, and one hundred and twenty gallons of strong beer were given to the people of Greenham Mill. The colour of the coat was described as dark Wellington, the cloth was Hunting Kersey. Kersey itself is usually described as a coarse woollen material. It was my guess that Hunting Kersey would have been a very robust cloth, probably thorn if not bullet-proof.

'Well, thass a rum'un,' remarked Jethro, 'You didn't say nothing about the wool being scoured so I reckon that jacket smelt wholly rural.'

The dipping was in full swing when I arrived. Half the flock were standing in a resentful huddle, dripping gently, shaking themselves from time to time and no doubt contemplating the indignities to which they had just been subjected. The remainder were in a holding pen from which they were released two at a time and urged energetically towards the dipping trough. They were an obstreperous lot. One could imagine that they knew very well what they were in for and were trying their best to avoid taking the plunge. Every single one had to be urged to the brink and pushed in.

To be fully effective total immersion is necessary, so each one had to be pushed under with a long-handled dipping crook, before being allowed to scramble up the ramp to rejoin those who had already suffered. The smell of 'dip' was not too unpleasant but all-pervasive. Everyone engaged in the work was wearing protective clothing. I wasn't, so I didn't get too involved.

As the last sheep emerged Jim said to William, 'While we're at it, you'd best go and get your little lot and we'll put them through.' William shot off down the lane and was soon back with his half-dozen in the trailer. He backed skilfully into the open gateway of the holding pen, lowered the ramp of his trailer and said, 'Come on, girls.' Now, William's sheep had all been hand-reared and tended to regard him as their leader and father-figure. They came out obediently from the trailer and followed him to the dipping trough. At the last moment William stepped aside and they all went on into the dip one after the other. I don't think they would ever have fully trusted him again.

Outside the workshop at Ford Farm William has a traditional shepherd's hut. Mounted on iron wheels, it can be towed gently and noisily, in the absence of any sprung suspension. Though not as picturesque as a gypsy caravan, it nevertheless has an uncertain charm and immediately evokes thoughts of a pastoral scene. According to the time of year one might envisage the shepherd emerging from it into worsening weather, to bring in his flock to the shelter of a fold already built of bales of straw, or more happily starting off on his rounds to attend to the needs of newborn lambs and their mothers.

In fact the life of a shepherd can be very hard and demanding, not always as depicted by poets. For a touch of realism I like to recall the often told story about Mary's grandmother, who is reputed to have said, 'Just look at those little lambs, dear, aren't they beautiful? I do like a nice piece of roast lamb.'

The inside of William's hut is becoming as one might have expected to find it when in use. One of the difficulties when one deals in bygones is trying not to allow oneself to keep all the best and most interesting items. In the field of shepherding William allows a little self-indulgence. In a corner of the hut there is a charming little solid fuel stove. A stove-pipe goes up through the roof. The bunk at the far end from the stable-type door is built over a hutch in which a sickly lamb might be bedded down. There is a flap table on one of the walls. On this and hanging from the walls are the tools of the trade: crooks, knives, shears and bottles, a couple of smocks and a hat. I am not sure if the hat really belongs to the collection, as I have certainly seen William wearing it.

This weekend the public were invited to go and see the lambs and the daffodils up at the Hall, with an additional lure of rides in a tractor-drawn trailer round the estate. The event was in aid of the Red Cross. There was almost a feudal air as we, the villagers, trooped up the long drive to the Hall. The sun shone, the daffodils danced, the lake glittered and the children had a wonderful time bottle-feeding and caressing the lambs.

Quite a different entertainment was on offer some years ago when Mary and I were up in Yorkshire. A poster caught my eye, and, like any good one of its kind, it drew me across to read more. 'A sheep-shearing contest, Saturday 17th, 2.30 pm. In aid of the Recobble the Square Fund.' So, the following afternoon, we joined the crowd to watch the contest. It was noticeable that the crowd appeared to be made up mainly of visitors, like ourselves. No doubt sheep-shearing has been going on so long in the Dales that even a contest will attract only limited local interest.

The running commentary was given by a Young Farmer whose organisation had arranged the event. He did it extremely well. His nice earthy sense of humour was backed by his knowledge of sheep, of wool and of the competitors. His voice and accent were charmingly in accord with the subject and the setting of a moist afternoon in the market place at Grassington. One thing is certain. Never again will I pronounce that name with the long 'a' of a southerner. Not, mind you, that I count myself a southerner – I am an East Anglian, which is something different again.

The first contestants took their places in the roped-off centre of the square just above the pump. These three young men were wearing a strange assortment of gear but each had a great air of self-assurance, not ill-placed, and a bright pair of shears, brighter by far than any I have handled in the workshop. Each contestant sheared three sheep, collecting them from and returning them to a holding pen. Each fleece was rolled into a tight bundle.

The standard was high, and when the judges announced the result only three points separated the winner from his rivals. Those judges, too, clearly knew their business – they had that quiet air of confidence bred from a sure knowledge of what one is about. Their task was no easier with the second lot of contestants. These were men with more years and experience behind them of practical and competitive work. It is always a joy to watch craftsmen at work and these were surely leaders in their craft. There was artistry in the sheer competence and economy of their movements; a poetry of motion in the rhythmic hiss of their shears. There was something like magic too. In a matter of short minutes rather tatty Wensleydales were transformed into clean attractive animals. They seemed to shed their cares and age as their fleece was removed like a single garment. There are few less dignified moments for sheep than when they are inverted and in the firm grip of a shearer, but once shorn and back on their feet they quickly regain their composure.

In all, it was a well-staged show and I hope that contributions to the fund matched the applause and that the square got recobbled.

On one of his rare visits to Ford Farm my brother-in-law registered a small triumph by counting the sheep thus :

'Yan, tan, tethera, pethera, pimp.'

Luckily there were only five in sight, as I believe that to have been the sum total of his knowledge of country lore. He did admit to being unable to remember the further fifteen numerals to make the score. Even so I think it was quite a feat to have remembered that much, learned from a shepherd many years previously on a holiday in Devon.

LOT 4
Wheeling and Dealing

Of all the farm sales that I have attended, one stands frozen in my memory. The morning was so cold that all our efforts to get warm by working hard had failed. Eventually William said, 'We could go over to Hethersett for the sale, it can't be much colder than this'. For once he was wrong! In spite of the amazing assortment of clothes we put on, we never did get warm.

We were surprised by the number of vehicles in the field set aside for parking. I thought that the field would be turned into a sea of mud, but it had been well chosen, a well-drained slope down to a little stream which immediately clicked in my memory as the source of water for the water-jump at pre-war Hethersett Races. My Aunt Ethel used to take me there. I didn't in those days know much about betting on horses, yet even then it struck me as strange that she always insisted on putting money on the first horse she saw on the day. Perhaps it was a system as good as any.

There was a good crowd inspecting the lots laid out on the grass. We might have been conspicuous in our outlandish dress, but this was far from the case; everyone was well protected against the icy blast, and we huddled together like cattle for mutual protection. William had a catalogue so knew he would be interested in only the first dozen lots to be offered. The ringing of a handbell drew the crowd to Lot No.1.

Sad items of deadstock were lined up on the wet grass; three lots of metal pigsty doors, a dubious-looking force-pump and sundry objects which I could not identify. William had three lots knocked down to him: a hay rake, three churns and a pig feeding trough. We all moved on in a milling crowd to Lot No. 12. This was an ancient seed drill, about twelve feet wide, standing on wheels four feet high. William estimated the piece at a generous bracket of between ten and forty pounds. He got it for eighteen, and the crowd moved on.

Up till then only the elements had presented problems. Now we had one of our own making. Having bought the thing, how were we going to get it home? On that bleak, wind-swept hillside, with an occasional flurry of snow about our ears, we set to and stripped it down. Improvising a cart-jack we raised one end at a time and removed the wheels. These were in fact the prime reason for buying the drill. However, piece by piece and with some loss of skin we struggled it all into the van and drove home.

You can always sell good cartwheels. Not surprising really, as they are such beautiful examples of good craftsmanship, redolent of nostalgia and fit to decorate the most gracious of patios or the most humble cottage. I am happy to record that after receiving tender loving care in our workshop, the subsequent sale of those wheels more than justified the whole unforgettable exercise.

Although this was by no means a typical day, it goes a little way towards answering a question I am often asked: 'Where do you do all your buying?' Of course I don't actually do any of the buying these days, which is just as well, because I am so horrified by prices now that I would find it very difficult. In fact, the answer to the question is very much as it would have been in our days at the Old Forge, when Mary was our chief buyer and William and I got out and about only occasionally. 'Anywhere and everywhere' is the answer, or as the Duke of Wellington would say, 'Never miss an opportunity'.

It is possible to go to an auction sale almost every day of every week within a radius of about forty miles. Most of them are regular events, in what used to be market towns, on what used to be market day. If the cattle and sheep pens are now missing, the street market stalls still appear regularly, and the auctioneers confine themselves to 'deadstock' and household goods.

'One-off' sales, such as farm sales or the now rare 'country house sale' are advertised in the local paper, and while looking for them the Miscellaneous Articles for Sale columns are always worth a few minutes during the morning coffee break. It is comparatively rare for us to buy from shops or antiques centres – far better as a rule to acquire items when they first come on to the market, rather than having passed through other hands where each time someone will have taken a profit. We have one good friend whom one might describe as a runner. He brings offerings from time to time. I thought that I had disguised him thoroughly when I wrote about him in *A Living in the Past*, but he saw through the disguise, so I will say no more.

Although William doesn't take on house clearances, he does help another dealer with them from time to time. I sometimes get roped in, as happened on that occasion at Rectory Farm. In house clearances or removals there is usually an old chap to be seen carefully wrapping and packing china and glass – that's me! I'm still quite capable of giving a hand with the furniture, but am increasingly treated with the consideration my years have earned me. The arrangements made over house clearances vary considerably according to the situation, but usually yield financial reward and some stock, in varying proportions.

The clearances themselves are as diverse as the human race. I remember an immaculate bungalow where there was not a speck of dust behind the piano, and everything in the kitchen was spotlessly clean. In total contrast, I recall a cottage where one felt like donning rubber gloves, and where one would have been sorry to have housed a pig. Equally unlike that exemplary bungalow was an unforgettable apartment on two floors above a shop – up two narrow flights of stairs from a rear entrance off a courtyard, which was just being paved, and over which everything had to be carried to the van out in the street. The worst items there were three night storage heaters. They were so impossibly heavy that we had to take the backs off and carry the bricks two at a time. We were also obliged to remove a window frame on the top floor to enable us to lower two pieces of furniture on a rope down to the busy street. I have often asked myself how the furniture got up there in the first place.

On another occasion we were frustrated by an armchair which had been reupholstered, making it just a few inches too big for straightforward removal. Big storage cupboards which have been built or rebuilt in situ are not uncommon; they are best looked at with one's blind eye and left severely alone. Don't talk to me about pianos.

At times one begins to feel one has seen everything, and then something quite amazing turns up. Clearing the furniture from a house in Pakefield, we noticed a large, dark stain on the dining room ceiling. Somewhat sinister, it was neither black nor brown but a reddish hue in between. Rather cautiously we went upstairs. In the bedroom we found two motorbikes. A corpse would have been less surprising, and easier to get downstairs. The water-cooled Scott and Harley-Davidson were worth more than all the furniture put together.

I recall another nasty smear of similar colour caused by a tin of Tate and Lyle black treacle, which had rusted through, and which left a sticky trail all the way from the larder and down the front steps to the van.

A nice little farmhouse in North Norfolk produced an early jolt to dislodge any tendency towards blaséness. The layout of the building puzzled us, as there seemed to be more rooms upstairs than down. The answer to our enquiry was, 'Oh, yes! We papered over the door to that room; Mother didn't have no further use for it'. We wondered what happened to Father and didn't like to ask.

Over at Stonham Aspell we nearly had two nasty accidents in the space of a few minutes. We walked into one room where we suddenly realised that we could see still, dark water through the gaps in the floor. On the far side of the room there was a pine chest of drawers. We nearly went through the rotting floor to get to it, and when we moved it a large portion of the clay-lump wall collapsed into the water. On another occasion the presence of water, this time in the cellar, was brought to our notice in a house near Boxford. As we were removing furniture to the van we heard a motor cutting in and out. We asked what it was and were told that it was an electric pump in the cellar, which cut in automatically when the water level rose.

Not far from Eye we saw our first example of an al fresco bathroom. I don't think there was any hot water laid on, but otherwise it appeared to be complete. At the same house the ceiling in the kitchen was so low that neither of us could stand upright, all at variance with the grand staircase with mahogany banisters, the beautifully moulded coving in the main rooms and the valuable antique furniture.

There is, I am sure, a word for what I can only describe as a visual cliché. In this area one has often heard or read of someone keeping money under the mattress. As often as not a newspaper report describes how some unfortunate person has had life savings stolen from such a cache. Towards the end of the twentieth century one wouldn't think anyone could be so foolish. Well, they can! William and I were helping with a house clearance not very far from home. When we stripped the very ancient mattress off a bed there was a tin cash box – black and decorated in gold, with brass handles. 'Be funny if there was money in it,' we agreed, and there was! Forty pounds, to be exact, and it had been there a good many years as the fivers were all of the previous issue. Finders keepers? Porter's perks? Well, no, the old chap had been moved into a home, and his need was clearly greater than ours.

Occasionally, at the end of one of those house clearing jobs, I get a small benefit in kind - anything from a portable radio to a handful of ball-point pens. (The one with which I am writing has 'Saga' emblazoned on it.) The latest in this line of unconsidered trifles was a Slumberland mattress. William gave us a hand to fight it up our cottage staircase and we left it standing between our bedroom and the bathroom. It looked huge, and so daunting that we couldn't immediately face the job of changing it for the old one on our bed.

On Friday we woke up feeling strong and tackled the job. We struggled with the old mattress, and pushed it down the stairs, where it stuck. The only way to get down was to use it like a chute. From there we dragged it into the yard where, by chance, we met the dustmen. At this point I put on an act and became a rather pathetic old chap who couldn't think what to do about an unwanted mattress. What ought I to do about it? Was there some Council office from where I could seek advice? Was there a special collection service for such articles? They took pity on me, those fine strong upstanding men. 'Don't you worry,' they said, 'we'll soon take care of that'. They picked up the mattress and with one standing at each end, slung it into their machine. It wasn't quite as spectacular as the time we saw our old chest freezer flung into a similar gaping maw. It was ingested with a loud 'flump' followed by silence. One felt quite sad.

LOT 5
Time marches on

'Hold your head up and pull your shoulders back!' – faint echoes of the Drill Sergeant on the parade ground in the Royal Citadel. In fact it was the gentle voice of 'the one I love best', softly reminding me to watch my posture and remember my grandfather.

At the age of 80, Colonel Hill still walked to his office in Opie Street. I could just as well say marched, as he still retained his upright military bearing. At that time I considered this to be pretty remarkable. Now it seems rather less so and I would have no difficulty in walking daily to my office if I had one. What my grandfather did when he got to his office I do not know; perhaps he read the paper, went out for coffee at L.O.C. in London Street and then home for an early lunch. Or perhaps I do him an injustice.

The last time I saw him sitting at his desk he mistook me for my cousin Peter. I was a bit miffed by such an error but with the passing of time I now appreciate how easy it is to make such mistakes and to be prey to a leaky memory.

In 1940, when I was off to the war, my grandfather proposed giving me a hip flask, which he evidently considered to be essential equipment for a young officer. I persuaded him that a wrist-watch would be much more useful and happily he agreed. It was a good watch. It served me well through sandstorms in the Middle East, the siege of Malta, the jungles of West Africa, only giving up when immersed in the placid waters of Tarkwa Bay.

I bought a replacement in Lagos which also served me well for several years. I ought to have learned my lesson and bought one which was water-proof because I eventually capsized a 14-foot dinghy on Oulton Broad and that was the end of watch number two.

Number three I am wearing at this time. It isn't actually mine; it belongs to my brother-in law. He is a very particular sort of chap, a former Royal Engineer. He had two watches, both of which he kept wound up, as one should. When I heard of this I offered to look after one watch for him and that is how the matter stands at the present (correct) time.

Like its predecessors, this is a reliable watch which has never let me down. The ludicrous fact that Mary and I missed the ferry from Corfu to Paxos was no fault of the watch. I was entirely to blame for not having altered it to local time when we arrived on the island.

Towards the end of the war I had been transferred from the Gunners to Infantry. Given the choice of regiments I naturally elected for the Royal Norfolks. Not that it made the slightest difference, I was immediately posted to the Royal West African Frontier Force in Nigeria and finished up in India.

When my grandfather retired and relinquished command of the 1st Volunteer Battalion Norfolk Regiment the sergeants presented him with a Black Jack, a handsome silver-mounted drinking vessel which now stands on my desk. The only symbol to mark my time in the army is a Malta George Cross 50th anniversary medal. Of course time had marched on fifty years before this was struck. My father outshone both of us; he was awarded the Military Medal.

Such personal memories are often stirred by the watches, medals or old photograph albums which pass through our hands. What stories lie behind them – whole lives that we can only guess at.

Alphabet of Advice for Antiques-lovers

Amber – Wash in warm milk. Visit Southwold.

Bamboo furniture – difficult to repair. Elaborate pieces desirable.

Cane seating – cost of replacement to be weighed against total value.

Dressing chests – may require work on runners. A touch of wax will aid smooth running.

If Enamel conjures visions of kitchenware, forget it and move on to Russian silver gilt or Viennese exotics.

Furniture fashions change; follow your own preference.

LOT 6
Pastorale

The gate and its posts were made of tubular steel, clearly a first class engineering job, and just as clearly following a traditional design for a five-barred gate. Although not entirely acceptable to an old romantic, I have to say that it was smooth, delightfully sun-warmed and exactly the right height to be leaned on.

My contentment was invaded by a horrid thought. Was this the new standard Euro-gate which would finally sweep away all local variations of style? There was a time when one could judge perhaps not the county but the region in which one was by the form of the five-barred gates. This applied so long as gates were made by local or estate carpenters. Local traditional patterns started to disappear with mass-production. Since then the increasing width of farm vehicles and machinery has meant that many beautiful gates have disappeared – too small for the job and too big to become collectors' pieces.

William and I had paused to watch hay-making in progress. The greater part of my knowledge of agriculture derives from holidays in the Twenties and Thirties spent at Hollybush Farm in Staffordshire, where my friend Geoffrey and I used to go and stay with his uncle, usually around haymaking or harvest time. Uncle Jim and Aunt Cissy must have been very tolerant people, as I can't imagine we were a great help at such a busy period. Decades later, here in front of us was a scene which, though undeniably haymaking, was different in almost every detail from those far-off days.

In the business of antiques and bygones we handle a fair number of wooden hayrakes and the full range of hayforks. Neither of these tools was in evidence in the scene before us. An impressive tractor was towing a tedding machine, the whirling machinery leaving regimented swathes of turned hay. The pleasant sight was accompanied by the heady scent which hung in the air.

I must suppose that in these days of high technology and mechanisation there are still moments in every agricultural operation which require human judgement. I can well remember Uncle Jim studying the weather and deciding when it would be right to cut the hay. Haymaking more than any other operation requires the co-operation of the elements. His next moment of judgement came when deciding if the time was right for turning (or tedding) the mown hay. If the weather was unkind this might need to be done more than once, and in extreme conditions could result in total failure. Then came his final moment of decision. It was almost like a religious rite seeing him lift a handful, feel it for texture, look at it for colour and bury his nose in it for a good sniff. If the verdict was yes, we all pitched in to gather and cart the hay to the place chosen for the stack, which was usually near the field gate. Stacking was not a job for schoolboys or amateurs. Aunt Ellen and the other womenfolk were all conscripted for haymaking, it so often being a race against time. They customarily wore straw hats or bonnets to protect their complexions. I used to think they looked rather formal, more as if dressed for church than for working in the fields.

It used to be said that no good farmer would ever sell his hay, the thinking being that it should remain on the farm to be fed to the stock in winter and eventually be returned to the land to maintain fertility, mixed with the straw trodden down in stockyards. I remember hearing of an exciting exception to this rule, though sadly I was never there at the right time to participate. It seems that every year a circus came to town. The arrival of this entertainment was prefaced by the appearance of a flamboyant character who arrived on a piebald horse. Each year he did a deal with Uncle Jim for the supply of a quantity of fodder, and the deal always included free seats in the Big Top.

But we have left those stalwarts in the hayfield at Hollybush building a stack just inside the gate. I believe that building a haystack is even more skilful than building a straw stack, where the straw is delivered to the rickmaker in sheaves. Or rather, I should say, used to be delivered in sheaves, as the only sheaves around today are where a crop has been specially harvested for a thatcher. The stuff ejected from a combine harvester is of no use to that craftsman. Whichever sort of rick was being constructed it was very much a matter of teamwork, sweat and toil. The final skill required was putting on a thatch to protect the rick until the hay was required. At that point those amazing wide-bladed hay knives would be brought into action. It was not the custom in those parts to build ricks up on those mushroom-like staddle-stones which are now more often bought and sold as garden ornaments.

Another happy thing I remember is that if one was lucky enough to be around at threshing time one could always be sure of a good rat hunt with the dogs around the rick-yard, as well as all the excitement of the steam traction engine and the threshing machine.

What I didn't learn about haymaking and harvesting as a boy I have learned many years later by sitting quietly in the pub listening to my betters. I have realised that among other things I was slightly mystified when I had seen haystacks being thatched with straw. It had not then occurred to me that hay was useless as a thatching material and that the straw being used had been saved from the previous year especially for the job. There were, of course, many things going on around the farm which I accepted as a matter of course, never thinking to question the reason for doing things a certain way. In most cases I am sure that, had I questioned the reason, the answer would have been 'Because that's the way Father always done it'.

We don't have many thatcher's tools through our hands. They are rather basic, and even a leggat, which might be regarded as a 'conversation piece' is not exactly a thing of beauty.

William and I had stopped that day to eat our lunch after making a delivery at Stoke-by-Clare. It was a relatively easy delivery. (Any midwife will agree that some are more difficult than others). The big pine dresser was heavy, but with the top removed, drawers taken out and an easy access to the kitchen it had presented no special difficulties. Nor was it difficult to see where it had to stand. There was only one place where it fitted. We could also see why our customer had been so particular about measurements, even requiring us to reduce the height by a couple of inches (5cm). There was just one snag. When in position against the wall the dresser masked the electric light switch. After some discussion it was decided not to call in an electrician to move the switch but to have a hole cut in the back of the dresser. Now, it may sound like vandalism to do such a thing but the back was only lightweight tongue and groove, and someone in the distant future would be able to make good if required. So, out came the tool-bag, which experience has taught us to have available on any such expeditions, and we cut a square hole to frame the switch on the wall.

We knew those upper reaches of the River Stour from when we were at the Old Forge, so remembered a good place to stop for our picnic, from where we had a good view down the valley. It was from there that we had seen the haymaking in progress and had gone down for a closer look. The valley offers a pastoral scene as satisfying as one could wish for. The railway, which might have wrought some desecration, has come and gone (arrived and departed, as they would say), allowing the valley to revert to a tranquil beauty of Constable quality.

We found it very easy to rest in the warm sunshine and relax for a spell, with our feeling of comfort enhanced by having just folded and put a handsome cheque in one's back pocket. A remark to kill romance, maybe, but even though we enjoy our work it is not an end in itself.

LOT 7
Al fresco

'If you've got to work,' said William, 'there can't be conditions much more pleasant in which to do it'. It was a perfect day, warm sunshine and a gentle breeze. We had moved out of the workshop and were working on a makeshift bench in the shade of a maple tree. William had planted the sapling not long after moving to Ford Farm.

The proposition having being carried nem. con. we proceeded to gild the lily, suggesting ideas which could possibly improve our situation. It would be nice, we agreed, to have the stream a little closer. We have such happy memories of the Chadd brook which flowed only a few feet from our workshop at the Old Forge, and have to admit that we spent quite a lot of time looking out of the window at the passing scene, the wildlife and our own geese who patrolled the banks and put on aquatic displays for our pleasure. But there we had no panoramic view of lakes and woodland and the noisy A134 was only yards away beyond the willow trees.

The slightly off-beat job we were on this particular morning was the restoration of a number of sheep hurdles. Now, you might not immediately think of wooden hurdles as being desirable bygones. I confess that I was a little sceptical but have now learned to have complete faith in William's judgement of the market place. These rather charming objects are so clearly the work of craftsmen, and not having even a nodding acquaintance with the machinery of mass-production, I now see them in a variety of garden situations.

The sight of those hurdles took my mind right back to those bad old days of straw and stubble burning. One of our farming neighbours let the flames get a little out of control and took out about twenty feet of hedgerow. I ordered some mixed hedging stock from the garden centre and prepared the ground. To keep our geese in and also to protect the young hedge from the wind we thought that we would get some wattle hurdles.

'Old Fred's the man', said Norman, our postman, so off we went to look for Old Fred, and found him in his big shed beyond his hazel plantation. We told him our plan.

'Ah!' says he. 'What you don't want is garden hurdles. You want sheep hurdles, and that's a funny thing because I don't make many of them these days'.

He explained that sheep hurdles are about 42 inches high, while garden hurdles are more like six or even eight feet high. He was really rather pleased to have an order for sheep hurdles, which he said were in steady demand when he started working with his father. Fred and now his son, Billy, had diversified into basketry. This had meant moving into a range of different materials including imported cane, local willow, hazel and chestnut. He also added weight to one of my theories about ancient crafts being littered with obscure terminology, using such words as 'bolts', 'upsetting', 'waling' and 'randing'. Rather as in my occasional occupation of rush seating, some of these terms probably date from Biblical times.

I am thinking of Moses' mother, who you will recall 'took for him an ark of bulrushes and daubed it with slime and pitch and put it in the flags by the river's brink'. I strongly suspect that some distortions took place in the translation of that passage. Pitch I can go along with, but slime? Confusing bulrushes, flags and reeds is perpetuated to this day by the compilers of crossword puzzles. A thatcher has no use for rushes and a basket-maker will get nowhere with reeds.

While we have a Bible in our hands we may note a number of references to reeds, in particular 'a golden reed' for measuring – and I confess that there I am in the dark.

When Fred was called away to attend to another customer, Billy was delighted to take centre stage and tell us what it was like working with his father.

'Proper ole slave driver he were when I started on basket work. He kept trashing my efforts until we had near on a shedful of what he said weren't no use to nobody. Now I'm better than what he is, though I doubt that he'd ever allow so. Even while I've been in the trade things have changed a lot. We did have a good line in laundry hampers, 27 inches by 18 by 12 they was, but the market for them dropped off very quickly and we had to think more of decorative sorts of baskets. Even shopping baskets went dead when them supermarkets come along and dish out plastic bags. I expect he'll put me on to making those sheep hurdles for you and I'll have to put up with a lot of old squit about the fabulous speed at which he used to make 'em'.

I asked if he or his father had ever tried his hand at making trugs. This was clearly outside his ken. It is probable that this particular skill is not found much beyond the bounds of Sussex, where it is an ancient craft and the materials readily available locally. The price of these desirable articles, new or second hand, has come a long way since they were strictly utilitarian, even being used for carrying coal – a far cry from elegant lady gardeners cutting a few roses or a bundle of asparagus.

None of which has anything to do with the hurdles on which William and I were working! These were the other sort, rather like miniature five-barred gates, made largely of chestnut, light, easily transported and remarkably strong. We cannibalised two of them to provide replacement pieces for the remainder. Although very much individuals, the dimensions of the parts were remarkably precise so that their interchangeability made our work relatively easy.

The bonus of a hot day with a good drying breeze is the ease with which items such as these hurdles or baskets can be pressure washed and dry within hours, instead of hanging around for days as can happen in winter. Eventually William and I moved back into the workshop, leaving the washed hurdles to dry in the sunshine. It is amazing how many tools accumulate on what may have looked like a simple job. All the small ones went back into the set of oak drawers, the ones which my father-in-law salvaged when they were being thrown out of the Bank of England (another rather nice piece of provenance to mention casually, together with the fact that he made our bedside table with oak from the same source.)

Our next task was preparing the load for Sunday's Antiques Fair at Hingham. This is not entirely straightforward. William has moved on from the big white van to a large Volvo Estate with a commensurately large roof-rack; the sort of vehicle that we used to refer to as a 'typical dealer's car'. Well, if you can't beat 'em join 'em.

That roof-rack can accommodate amazing loads. Recently we dismantled a sectional shed. The sections proved to be about the limit of our combined lifting power. We got them all on to the roof-rack, and all the shed contents inside. But of course without the van, weather becomes a crucial factor, furniture being more susceptible to damage than garden sheds, so choices have to be made. At the same time it is necessary to try and picture how the stand can be built up to give maximum visual impact and interest: 'Yes, you'd better wax polish the back of that piece, it will show on the stand!' William is remarkably good at the three-dimensional thinking which is needed when packing the maximum possible amount of furniture and other items into or on top of a vehicle. I think he honed these skills some years ago when working for a furniture removal firm.

If pressed, we can all confess to experiences with ill-secured loads on roof-racks. Our best story on that subject was told to us by a cousin of Mary's, the one who had a serious antiques establishment in Sheffield. Coming down the M1 he saw a nice little bow-fronted chest of drawers on a roof-rack. As he came alongside he saw the drawers starting to lift, then one by one they flew out. Luckily for him, the wind blew them on to the hard shoulder. As he said, he had often referred to a nest of drawers, but had never previously seen them leave the nest.

What other jobs were we doing that morning before we moved inside? As far as I remember we dealt with a small pine table of which the two top sections had shrunk to leave a gap down the middle. We rectified this and then enjoyed dealing with another of those splendid carpenters' chests. I don't think that they were ever mass-produced. Each one has its own features, some more elaborate than others, and always variations in the internal arrangement of drawers, slides, fittings and fixtures.

I'm fairly sure it was that morning when we worked on a wooden wheelbarrow. The geometry of wheelbarrows is interesting; there isn't a right-angle anywhere, which means that very careful measurement is needed when cutting a replacement part. As always it is desirable to match the original wood as closely as possible.

I also recall that in the course of the morning we moved round the tree, keeping in its pleasant shade, which indicates to me that one may plant oak trees for one's great-grandchildren, while acers may be planted for one's own pleasure.

LOT 8
Mills and Bills

'It's the special Bygones Sale next month', said William. 'Better sort that lot out ready to take in on Monday'.

'Sorting that lot out' is always an occupation which I enjoy, for among what one might call regulars there are always two or three items of more than usual interest. On this occasion the regulars included a range of tools from various trades: carpentry, cabinet-making, lead work, masonry and manufacturing processes such as brick-making, thatching, cheese-making and smithing.

Most of these tools are generally recognised, some are beautiful and some are just curious. The visual impact of each and every one is hugely enhanced by careful and sympathetic cleaning. There is tactile pleasure in holding a well-balanced tool with its handle smooth-worn by use – a flail is a classic example of this.

For me the special treats are the more obscure or rare tools which sometimes defy identification without reference to William's extensive reference library. I was puzzled recently by one item, partly because it was out of context among wooden shoe lasts, a carpet-stretcher, milliner's blocks and a pair of three-legged stools. (Have you ever seen a one-legged milking stool? The only one I have seen was shaped like a table-tennis bat with the single leg at the centre.) If there had been anything to suggest milling I ought to have recognised a mill-bill, which is used by a millwright for dressing the stones.

When I was at Letheringsett, the miller told me that in the absence of a local millwright he dresses his own stones. He showed me a selection of 'bits' which can be inserted into the wooden handle, and also his 'proving staff' with which he checks that his dressing is even.

My interest in mills and milling started early in life, which was not surprising as my father worked for Colmans of Norwich. My friend Geoffrey and I used to visit Keswick Mill, and we once spent a week at Saxlingham. Also, during our stays at his uncle's farm, we always visited his other uncle, Reuben, at his watermill.

More recently than those far-off days before World War 1, Mary and I actually lived in a windmill. We were selling our old farmhouse near Worstead, and in order to give quick vacant possession and clinch the sale, we stored the furniture in the barn and proposed to live in our caravan. By chance, some good friends offered us the temporary use of their windmill. I cannot wholeheartedly recommend such a home, but it was certainly an interesting and informative interlude.

Some years ago I found my way back to Staffordshire and took Mary to meet my old friend. It wasn't easy; the area had changed a lot. The local telephone directory still listed 'Noden, R. Mill Farm'. I rang the number. 'This is David Hill, you won't remember me. You will remember your nephew Geoffrey. We came to stay with you when we were boys'. A breathless pause, then, 'Oh yes, I do remember you. You must be quite an old boy now. I pulled you out of the millpond; you got into a lot of trouble about that'.

We soon got to Mill Farm following his instructions. When I saw the place I began to recognise it, as memories and realities slotted into position. He met us in front of the house, this old friend, and I introduced Mary. We stood talking in the sunshine (funny how often the sun is shining in my memories.) Wisteria hung over the doorway and pears ripened against the sun-warmed stone. We reached back into the past, establishing a new adult relationship.

Quite soon we went inside. 'Feast your eyes', he said, 'while I go and make some coffee'. So while the kettle came to the boil on the range we looked around his home. It was truly a treasury of bygones. There were items of farm and dairy equipment, half-finished mechanical inventions which, had they been pressed to completion, might have brought him fame and fortune.

As we sat and sipped our coffee he told us sadly how he managed as a widower. His wife had died only the previous Spring. We spoke of his nephew Geoffrey who had been my closest friend until he was killed flying in the R.A.F. early in the war. There didn't seem to be many of us left to remember those early days on the farm.

Then Reuben showed us round. Strangely, I remembered little of the house. Perhaps as a boy one is not especially interested in beauty or domestic arrangements. The stream, millpond and the mill itself were another matter altogether. There I had total recall. We looked at everything, the huge cast-iron overshot wheel, the massive wooden drive-shaft, the wooden-toothed gear wheels, (apple wood for durability and quietness), the bins and hoppers and of course the two sets of stones. The climax came when our host pulled gently on a well-worn wooden lever. There was a sound of rushing water, and through a hatchway we saw the water cascading over the wheel. Slowly it began to turn. The whole mill came to life with a gentle rumble and a rhythmic 'plosh, plosh' deep down in the mill race. Oats jogged steadily down from above, while meal started flowing down the wooden chute to the floor below. It was a moment of magic connecting past with present.

All of which explains the pleasure to be derived from bygones and collectibles, especially when one is able handle them and recall personal involvement; then their worth suddenly becomes far greater than their intrinsic value. And I think that I may excuse myself for not immediately recognising that 'bill'. I have never actually seen a millstone being dressed – nor, for that matter, have I ever seen a one-legged milking stool being used.

The order of priority for work in the workshop on any Thursday is directed by the calendar and the imminence of the next regular event. A wide range of furniture and larger items can be offered at the auction sale, held on the first Sunday of every month. There is always a choice to be made between putting a piece in the auction or on the stand at an Antiques Centre. A compromise solution is to offer a lot for sale at a sensible reserve price, and then if that is not reached, to take it to Risby Barn, one of the Antiques Centres. We load the van, which is always an interesting exercise, needing the same sort of expertise as house clearances, not only in loading vans but also in manoeuvring large furniture down impossible looking stairwells and other tight places.

Anticipating the Antiques Fair on the third Sunday of the month requires more serious consideration and a larger proportion of 'small portables'. There is no strict date line at this particular fair, so collectibles are in order and the scope is unlimited. Being almost antique (but not collectible) myself, it never fails to surprise me to see so many things offered which I remember well as everyday articles in use in and around the house.

Who would ever have imagined that that old bull's head tin opener would become a valuable and desirable object? For a birthday treat I was allowed to choose the sweet for lunch, and always chose tinned pineapple chunks. I remember so well whacking the spike into the top of the tin to get the cutter started. The opened tin tended to have dangerously jagged edges, unlike those that I now see opened by an electrically powered opener. I ask myself: can our modern-day artefacts possibly gain interest and value with the passing of time? In most cases it seems not only unlikely but absolutely impossible.

Closely allied to the tin-opener is the bottle-opener or corkscrew. The latter, like Mr Heinz's products, seems to come in 57 varieties, with a price range which is breathtaking. The one I remember from my childhood was of the simplest design – a steel screw set in a wooden handle, but not, of course, just any old wooden handle – clearly pride had been taken in its simple but pleasing turning.

That, I think, is one of the keys to the intrinsic value of so many ancient artefacts, the pleasure which is given by craftsmanship, the choice of materials and the restrained ornamentation. Nowhere do I find these aspects more obvious than in woodworking and other hand tools. A Black and Decker power drill is an efficient tool, but will it be handled with pleasure and thought beautiful in a hundred years?

Naturally there was a big pine dresser in that kitchen of my early memories. I don't usually mention prices, as time changes values rapidly. I only note in passing that today the dresser would fetch about the same figure as that which Mary and I paid for our first house, £1,500.

We had a marmalade-cutter through the workshop recently; it lacked the wooden plunger used for pressing the oranges in against the revolving cutting blades. A replacement presented no difficulty with the lathe already set up, and a choice of suitable wood at hand. We didn't have a marmalade-cutter at home, but one used to make an annual appearance each January, which was when the Seville oranges came on the market. It was on loan from the shop where Mother bought the oranges, and was delivered with them by a boy on a bicycle.

Of course there was a coffee-grinder in the kitchen. It was fixed on one end of the dresser, and I must have been fairly small when I was allowed to use it, as I recall that to do so I had to climb up on cook's high-backed Windsor chair. I've long since lost count of the number of such chairs which have passed through our hands. They rarely fail to give me pleasure. Likewise the big pine tables on which we expend so much time and energy. The last one was just over seven feet long. Mercifully it had square tapered legs which are hugely easier to deal with than turned legs.

Almost everything in that kitchen and pantry would sit happily on a stall at a collectors' fair: stone hot-water bottles, flat irons, the big preserving pan, the mangle from the back kitchen and even the 'copper' itself, along with all the other small items such as butter-pats, wooden spoons, jelly moulds and most certainly the row of copper jugs which stood on the mantelpiece over the big black kitchen range – perhaps we can even include that in the list.

With the auction and the first fair over, there is little easing of the pressure for the next fair, which takes place on the fourth Sunday of the month. If you bear in mind that these three-monthly engagements come round remorselessly and that all the time there are the stands in the Barn and at the Antiques Centre to be supplied and serviced, you will appreciate that William is a busy man and that I am always conscious of the meagreness of my input.

While I am wandering round my childhood home I had better go upstairs, past the big oak chest and the linen press to my little room. There would be some treasures there; my Hornby trains, a portable gramophone – even the needle tins are collectors' items – a working model of a Lowestoft trawler and even my Box Brownie camera. We might even find a Codd's bottle complete with glass marble. I used to get these from the canteen at the Tennis Club beyond the bottom of the garden – threepence or fourpence, I think, and a penny back on the return of the empty (could be worth £100 today, but it's no use thinking of lost opportunities.)

Not very long ago we couldn't lay our hands on enough stools. The demand outstripped the supply, so of course prices went up and trade in them was reduced to a trickle. There is something rather attractive about stools, in the same way that the young creature is always more appealing than the adult, so perhaps one may subconsciously think that a stool will eventually grow up to become a chair! Certainly this has been the evolutionary route. In a house clearance with which William and I were assisting last week, I thought that I had spotted two potentially attractive stools. In both cases they turned out to be cut-down chairs, rather well padded and upholstered. One derived from the circular seat of an Ibex chair, the other from the even more familiar Windsor. Only rarely do we get involved with upholstery, but in the case of those two I would have hoped to be able to remove the upholstery and reveal two honest wooden stools.

It is true that I spent some happy afternoons attending upholstery classes in Lavenham, but I have rarely used the limited skills which I acquired. Only once have I tackled a job which required those ghastly spiral springs and endless stringing. I am fairly happy if pressed into the sort of job which requires only webbing, wadding and gimp. A good reason for avoiding re-upholstery work is that only by chance will one's choice of material agree with that of potential purchasers.

My earliest conscious memory of sitting on wooden stools goes back to schooldays, when we had tall stools in all the science labs – I can almost hear now the unpleasant shuddering noise they made when dragged across the tiled floors. Those stools were by no means new in those days so if they have survived they would sell well in any sale of bygones.

Sheffield and Horncastle were good sources of stools. When Mary and I visited our younger daughter and family we made a habit of shopping for them, and could rely on finding enough for their sale to cover our travelling expenses. The industrial stools in the Abbeydale Industrial Hamlet were the most coveted. I specially liked the ones on which the stretchers formed a cross, with one passing through the other.

Moving on to more elaborate versions, there is really no end to the number of styles that can be encountered; they range from good honest oak joint to elaborate creations from the remote corners of Empire, and, roughly speaking, the less useful they are the higher their price.

As a rather odd footnote, I mention that on more than one occasion I have wanted to buy a stool in a shop, only to be told, 'Oh, that's not for sale, we use it to reach the top shelf!'

---

*G*lass – the smallest of defects affects value. Dental cleaning tablets are very effective for cleaning glass.

*H*andles should always match the period of furniture. Reproductions are preferable to a mis-match.

*I*ndustrial memorabilia from dead or decaying industries are noteworthy.

*J*ade improves with handling.

*K*eys are desirable antiques. Replace missing keys.

*L*amps – a field of great interest. Even my desk lamp is an antique!

*M*etalwork should not invariably be cleaned. Be selective.

LOT 9
Great Raft Spider

'I'm not looking for perfection,' said William, 'but it would be nice if you could tidy them up a bit'. 'Them' was a disreputable looking bundle which, on investigation, turned out to contain three walking sticks, two umbrellas, one Chinese sunshade, two golf clubs and four carpet-beaters. From time to time I am given a little homework at the end of my weekly visit. This was one such occasion.

'Old walking sticks!' you say. 'Big deal.' But think again, a new one can easily set you back £24. Cleaning them presented no difficulty. The steel and brass ferrules polished up nicely, while the sticks themselves needed no more than a rub over with a soft cloth and just a suspicion of linseed oil. Like anything else you care to name, walking sticks are hugely collectable and the price range staggering. The most expensive one I have heard of fetched £3,400 – probably unique; it had a miniature camera built into its handle.

In the seventeenth and eighteenth centuries the walking stick was an essential fashion accessory for the man-about-town. It had taken a long time to achieve such status, when you consider that sticks and staves have probably been in use since man first stood on two feet.

Those three sticks that I was cleaning were good solid ash, much favoured by serious users and not aspiring to high fashion. From that starting point one can move on through an almost infinite catalogue of materials used: cane, rosewood, fruit wood, ebony, cabbage stalks, and various parts of animals and reptiles, to name only a few. Then one comes to the handles, which if not an integral part, may also be found to have been made from a similar variety of materials, ivory and horn probably topping the popularity chart.

I wonder what happened to my swagger canes. I had two; the first one had a silver top bearing the school crest, when I was in the O.T.C. The second was similar, with the Royal Artillery badge. I have just looked up 'swagger' in the *Oxford English Dictionary* and I cringe at the thought that I may have embodied the qualities associated with the word. Mention of the R.A. brings gun sticks to mind – rare and prized collectors' items, not to be confused with shooting sticks.

The umbrellas looked somewhat dejected – the word gamp came to mind – but they were intact. I opened them and gave them a good shower bath with the garden hose, which brightened things up considerably. They both had nice handles, so when dry and nicely furled no one could have dismissed them out of hand.

Chinese sunshades don't often come our way. I was a bit dubious about this one. However, I brushed it gently with a soft painter's duster and it began to look possible; no holes in the paper and nothing broken. After a bit of thought I sprayed it lightly with aerosol wax dressing, the same as one uses on Barbour jackets. The effect, if not actually electrifying, was very satisfactory.

I had to remind myself that wooden-shafted golf clubs are now relics of a bygone age. They responded to the same TLC as given to walking sticks, the faces of the irons burnishing up nicely with emery cloth.

By a process of natural selection I had left the worst job until last. I don't like working with cane, it entirely lacks tactile pleasure and can actually be positively unpleasant to handle. I never took to cane seating for that reason, as well as the fact that compared with rush bottoming or even sea grass working, the geometric precision required is not my style. Rushwork is therapeutic. Anyhow, there was no ducking it this time, three of the carpet-beater handles needed to be rebound, and sundry bits of the working parts needed remedial action. Happily I don't imagine that they will ever be used again for other than decoration. Naturally they set me thinking about that carpet-beating machine at Colchester, and the fact that it is a very long time since I last saw anyone beating a carpet; Mr Hoover, fitted carpets and more recently Mr Dyson, have eliminated that household chore. I remember it as a very regular feature of spring cleaning, together with another strange rite which consisted of dragging carpets, upside down, along the grass to clean them.

It is quite easy to find that, all unwittingly, you have the basis of a collection of walking sticks. There are worse thing s to collect. Almost every one is unique, even the standard ash stick will have its own variations provided by nature, and from there on the range is unlimited. No collection will be without a Swiss or Austrian example, emblazoned with heraldic shields which purport to prove that the owner has been to Bern, Luzern, Interlaken and the rest. (Been there, done that and got the tee shirt.) Not all will include those works of art favoured by shepherds and members of the royal family, those rather flamboyant jobs with handles carved from ram's horns. I did read that the E.U. was proposing legislation to ban these on the grounds that the horns might be infected with B.S.E., but there is absolutely no evidence that shepherd or members of the royal family actually chew the handles of their walking sticks.

On Tuesday, as usual, Mary and I went to the White Horse for lunch. With walking-sticks on my mind I was delighted to see two interesting examples. One actually has a name; it is called a Schafer stick and is, I believe, available through the N.H.S. The handle is made of plastic and looks somewhat like the ear of a strange animal; it is moulded to accommodate the whole palm of one's hand, and is thus able to take more weight than a normal handle. This is a strictly modern stick, but I am sure that is a collectable of the future.

The second stick was the first thing I noticed about Tom, who joined our table for lunch. He told me later that he was using it more from necessity than from habit or pleasure, as he was waiting for a hip replacement operation. The handle of his stick was fashioned into a dog's head, with two beady eyes inserted, giving it a very lively appearance. I hazard a guess that it was alder wood. He said that he had cut it down on the Fen many years ago, on Turf Night. He went on to tell me that Turf Night is an annual event, with origins lost in the mists of antiquity.

I was enchanted by the sound of this. Being a romantic soul, I could see myself poring over the parish records in a fever of research. I could almost smell the pervasive mustiness of the parish chest and feel the gentle crackle of parchment as I searched for the origins and early accounts of the event. Just the stuff, I thought, for an article in *Suffolk and Norfolk Life*, or one of the other glossy monthlies. Disappointment followed. Seemingly there are no written records. There is a strong suspicion that some existed until around the middle of the twentieth century, when they were destroyed after the death of the holder.

Happily the parishioners of Thelnetham have kept the event alive. Turf Night is a moveable feast, being linked to Easter, and takes place on the Monday following the Bank Holiday. Possibly its relation to the Church calendar indicates a very early origin.

The signal for action is the church bell, which is rung for five minutes in the evening. During these hectic minutes, any householder of the parish is entitled to step out a square of the Fen, marking the corners of the square with a spade. I am sure that in years past the spade would not have been of the garden variety but a traditional peat-cutter's spade, for one of the benefits to be gained is the right to cut peat from one's claim. I see no signs of recent peat digging. The other benefit is the right to cut wood, and of this Tom's walking stick is the only evidence I have seen.

Other informants have told me that only a small number of parishioners participate these days in keeping this delightful custom alive. It is easy to imagine that in years gone by the value of both peat and firewood must have engendered keen competition, undoubtedly leading to disputed claims and cases of 'fen rage'. These days, they say, we are more civilised. Although I am not entitled to step out a claim, I fully intend to be there for the next ceremony, and I think it highly probable that we will end up in the White Horse.

Mention of Redgrave and Lopham Fen reminds me of the time when I first heard of International Bog Day. Be honest, have you ever heard of it? Only by chance Mary had picked up a couple of leaflets the day before, which told us what would be happening down on the fen.

If you follow the road from Redgrave toward the Lophams, it drops gently down into a shallow valley. In a short distance it runs between alder carrs and silver birch trees; cool moist places on a warm summer's afternoon. The Ordnance map indicates that here are the sources of the Little Ouse and the river Waveney. Without that information one could easily miss them both, for there is nothing spectacular about them. There is no crystal clear spring rising like champagne among cool pebbles. Certainly there is no gushing water splashing into rock pools – I guess that the coralline crag of North Norfolk is the nearest rock to be found, and that is sixty miles away.

It is quite impossible to point and say, 'That is the source of the river,' for it is more of an idea, a gentle happening which occurs quietly among the lush greenery of this little fen, and away the two rivers flow in opposite directions. The Little Ouse gets away rather secretively among the trees. The Waveney immediately enters the glare of publicity, finding itself in an International Site of Special Scientific Interest.

I had not realised how many years had passed since I was last down on the fen. On that occasion David Bellamy was there. This time the Raft Spider took top billing. There were demonstrations of peat-digging (a more leisurely occupation than I had imagined!) sedge-cutting, wattle and reed fence-making and thatching.

An enormous amount of conservation work continues to be done. Intrusive scrub and trees are cleared, and dredging creates shallow lagoons and pits largely for those unique spiders, but also for many other forms of aquatic life. The spoil from such works is used to create walkways. I have to confess that I enjoyed the fen even more when it was less heavily managed and when one only occasionally met another bog lover. International Bog Day brought us out in considerable numbers.

When we lived at Redgrave the fen was almost at our doorstep. One of my favourite walks of an evening was along the woodland on the Suffolk side of the river to the sluice at the bottom end of the fen. Crossing over into Norfolk, I would then walk back towards the sunset and the source of the river beside the road. There was a feeling of timelessness, an illusion of being far from civilisation. There was peace and tranquillity, not silence, for even the lightest of airs would rustle the reed bed; there was bird song and the hum of insects, the swish of one's boots 'passing feather-footed through the plashy fen', and sometimes the scolding of a startled moorhen.

Choose your day and time with care, and blissful solitude can still be found on Redgrave Fen.

LOT 10
Collections

I was shocked this morning to find myself in the village shop asking for half a kilo of carrots. Perhaps I ought to have gone the whole way and asked for point five of a kilo. Either way, it caused me deep resentment to have been conned into an alien culture. There is a bright side; just think of all those weights and weighing scales which at a stroke have been consigned to the world of bygones! Even before Decimalisation Doomsday there was an interesting range of antique weights and measures for dealers and collectors to interest themselves in. Only last week William came back from a farm sale in deepest Suffolk with a bushel measure (36.40 litres). These wooden drums were customarily banded with a pair of iron handles set curiously low down, the reason being that they were less for carrying and more for tipping and emptying. The metal-rimmed top made sure of an exact quantity of grain being left in when the top was levelled off with a metal striker. Peck measures and their smaller brethren are not usually metal bound and are therefore more pleasing aesthetically. They are clearly closely related to articles made by the early American Shakers; cleaned and polished, they are highly desirable.

Unless you are a vintage car enthusiast you are not likely to be looking around garages for antiques and bygones, and even if you were, you might look for a long time before finding a set of copper, brassbound 'check pump' petrol measures. As the name implies, they were used for checking the accuracy of delivery from pumps. It would be nice to know that petrol pumps are checked for accuracy – one fills up with blind faith and has no means of making one's own check. I recall seeing only one set of these measures, and very handsome they are too. For some reason their squat appearance put me in mind of smugglers, not such a far-fetched idea as they were, of course, used by the Excise men.

You may be able to resist snapping up those 56lb weights from the sturdy weighing machines in the potato fields, but you cannot fail to be delighted with the beautiful bell-shaped weights from the butcher's shop or perhaps the Maypole Dairy. If you are old enough (almost a walking antique) you will remember standing with your nose just level with the marble counter, getting little drops of water splashed in your face as the assistant 'knocked up' half a pound of butter.

At the other end of the scale, if I may use the expression, there are those delightful letter scales on which letters can be weighed to establish correct postage. (In 1928 the standard rate was about one and a half old pence.) From around the same date I recall using scales in the laboratories with little slithers of metal for weights, which had to be handled with tweezers.

The range of ancient measures of length is as great as that of weights. Rods, poles and perches leap to mind, and surveyors' measures too – not those one-wheeled objects which men in yellow jackets push along the roadside, but the much older chain-links with brass tags.

If I pursued the subject of measures I am sure that I would find that almost every trade would reveal its own particular set, from Apothecary to Zeppelin manufacturer – a wide range for collectors and a rich field for wordsmiths. Who can resist those tables of weights and measures in the back of elderly encyclopaedias ? My favourites are :

Woolweights :	7 lbs	= 1 clove
	2 cloves	= 1 stone
	2 stones	= 1 tod
	6 ½ tods	= 1 wey
	2 weys	= 1 sack
	12 sacks	= 1 last.

Collecting mania has always been a bit of a mystery to me. No, I haven't forgotten those 32 hammers in the workshop, they are fully justified by the fact that over a period of time each one of them gets used for its specific purpose, except possibly the cobbler's, and that is so nice that it has earned honourable retirement.

You will realise that even if I don't understand the urge which spurs people on to make collections, I am more than happy to encourage such aberrations and to take a hand in providing what people want. The television programme 'Collectors' Lot' clearly demonstrates that it would be hard to find something which nobody collects.

I have news today of one of the regular 'Bygones and Collectibles' sales in one of our local salerooms. This sale is to include the entire collection from someone who specialised in all aspects of soap. What does one call such a person? Laundromaniac or detergentologist ?

No sooner had I mentioned house clearances than I was whisked off to another one.

'This will be an easy one,' said William. I didn't believe him, as I have yet to meet one answering the description. However, it was relatively easy. It was certainly the neatest, cleanest, tidiest home that we have encountered when assisting in these operations. There was really only one major snag. This was caused by the fact that a sun porch had been added to the bungalow doorway, which was just a few inches narrower than the original front doorway. Three-dimensional thinking was needed to get some of the furniture out, even after removing castors, covers or any other appendages.

The reason I mention this entertainment in connection with collectors is that among sundry sporting memorabilia and trophies there was a set of weight-lifter's gear, and in the china cabinets an extensive collection of commemorative mugs. Royal occasions were well represented, together with Pope John and a number of holiday destinations including the West Country, Malta, Canada and Scotland. And there I see a valid reason for making a collection. Many of the mugs were clearly souvenirs, reminders of happy times spent in pleasant places.

I wonder what happened to my matchbox collection – yes, I admit that I caught the bug at an early age but I got over it. Without doubt the collection became a war casualty together with my Hornby trains and Halford touring bicycle. That was my pride and joy – quite an advanced machine with drop handlebars, calliper brakes, an excruciating saddle and no gears. Its purchase was the result of my first raid on my East Anglian Savings Bank account. That too became a casualty of the war years. Its closure didn't yield enough to buy an engagement ring; I borrowed the balance required from my father and I'm not absolutely sure that I ever repaid the debt.

We have a friend who owns a truly remarkable collection of frogs. Not live ones – ceramic, wooden, metal, you name it, he's got it. The silly thing is that he doesn't really like frogs. The situation started when someone gave him a pair of undeniably beautiful ceramic frogs to which he gave pride of place in his sitting room. From then on it was assumed that he liked frogs, and he just can't stop people giving them to him. So beware, if you have two or more of anything you have the beginnings of a collection – better separate those garden gnomes before they start breeding.

When I was in the printing business it never occurred to me that any of the work that we turned out would ever be graced with the term 'Printed ephemera' and become sought after by collectors. But this was brought home to me when a number of auctioneer's posters came under the hammer. This particular batch consisted of what were known as 'poster particulars' which meant that they gave not just the what, where and when of the sales but also full details of the properties offered, together with the name and address of the solicitors. In one case this happened to be S. Garerd Hill and Sons, Opie Street, Norwich, my grandfather and uncles. As was the normal practice in the nineteen twenties and thirties, the posters were set with as many different typefaces as could be brought into play – in one instance sixteen.

You will realise if you have even a little knowledge of printing that I was a 'letterpress' printer, a fast disappearing breed swept away by the advancing tide of new technology. The machinery, tools and accessories of the old trade have become collectors' items, most notably the beautiful wooden block type used in poster printing as well as type-cases and the 'sticks' used by compositors. An Albion press is the acme of any collection. Printed ephemera covers a huge range: almost any matter which was clearly never intended to be retained, such as auctioneer's posters, tickets, programmes, leaflets, cigarette cards and postcards.

I could quite easily become a collector of picture postcards. I have a small volume of cards from the 'thirties and 'forties. In those days we didn't go around with cameras round our necks taking dozens of photographs instead of just looking at things. Picture postcards were in any case likely to be far better pictures of places than one could manage oneself. This little album contains four sets of cards, each of which represents a holiday. The first illustrates highlights from a walking tour in the Lakes in 1937. That was the last holiday I had with my father and he could still outwalk me. Second comes a group which starts with a vintage car making heavy weather of Parracombe Hill near Lynton, followed by three views of Lynmouth harbour with the Rising Sun Hotel prominent in the left foreground. Needless to say that was where we went for our honeymoon. I don't think that either of us had a camera at that time, and even if we had, films were hard to come by. The only snap we have from those idyllic days was taken by a friendly Polish airman who was also there on leave. The correspondence side of those cards, retrieved from the family, is predictably inconsequential.

The scene changes abruptly from the valley of the rocks and the White Lady to the bulb fields of Holland. The colourful pictures of the fields in Spring were not entirely true to our experience, as there was a late fall of snow that year, and we certainly ought to have had a camera to capture the strange scene. This was our first trip abroad after the war. Chocolate was still rationed at home but not, I note from the correspondence, in Holland. I remember that we sat on a seat in the gardens of the Kirkenhoff, where we were joined by a Dutch businessman who was anxious to exercise his English. He told us that he managed a chocolate factory, and would not allow his wife to eat chocolate 'because of her hippies'. We let no such consideration mar our enjoyment.

The next card in the album transports us to St Paul's Bay in Malta. If you know the place today you would not recognise the little fishing village that it still was in 1953. At that date there was only one hotel on the island! Rebuilding after the devastation of the siege years was well under way, and although I had thought that I would never wish to return after the war, this batch of cards recalls another blissful holiday.

The little album concludes with a return visit to the Lakes. By this time we were accompanied by three children and a Dalmatian. None of them appear on the postcards, we had got a camera by then – a Box Brownie, itself now also a collectible.

LOT 11
A good deal more

Two newspaper cuttings show me standing in the wreckage the morning after the fire. I don't think that 'sound-bite' or 'photo-opportunity' had entered the language at that time. I enjoyed very cordial relations with the local press; they were always pleased with a story and I wanted publicity. The reporters wouldn't have got anything very coherent out of me the evening before. It is a shattering experience seeing one's livelihood go up in flames.

We lost a number of quite amusing industrial antiques when the laundry was burnt down. Fearsome gas-heated irons, which must have been antiques even thirty years before, disappeared without trace. They were fuelled by the town's mains gas fed to them under pressure, the heat being controlled by a device similar to a Bunsen burner. Their one merit was that they heated up quickly and the heat was easily regulated. They were heavy, but anyone who uses an iron for several hours each day knows well enough to avoid lifting it more than absolutely necessary.

Associated with ironing there were crimping irons, goffering irons and a rather charming crimping machine, hand operated and heated by placing preheated rods inside its brass rollers. Those rods were heated over a normal gas ring. There were a variety of ironing boards of various shapes and large wickerwork trays in which stiff collars were placed. And of course there were hampers. I now see such hampers offered as bygones – they almost turn to ashes as I look at them and remember the column of smoke which Mary and I saw as we drove home from Norwich that fateful evening.

Among other trivia that went up in flames there was a short history of the company that I had written. The most memorable item I recall was a note recording the sale of the horse which used to draw the collection and delivery van, on the same day that the telephone was installed (Lowestoft 154).

We were out of production for the rest of the summer season. A lot of hard work by our staff and other people went into the rebuilding and re-equipping before we were again able to offer our services to a very loyal body of customers.

It would not be right to say that the event and its aftermath broke my back; it certainly killed my enthusiasm for the job. As soon as possible we sold the business and I was delighted to embark on a new life.

My new life didn't start right away. I am not ashamed to admit that I thoroughly enjoyed being unemployed. The feeling of release was enormous. Twice before, I had experienced a similar feeling. The first time was in the army when I was appointed to a staff job on General Christie's

38

staff. That was the first time since I had been an acting unpaid lance bombardier that I found myself without the responsibilities of leadership. The second time, also in the army, was sailing away to North Africa after three years besieged in Malta (1941, 1942, 1943).

I was never worried that I might not find myself a comfortable niche as I embarked on a series of interviews. The first one was hilarious. I had not adjusted to the fact that I was an interviewee, on the wrong side of the desk, so to speak. Eventually I was introduced to the principals of a small printing firm in North Norfolk, and shortly after that I note from my diary :

'I am now a Master Printer, a sufficiently ego-boosting title though on close inspection it turns out to be rather less grand than one might suppose. I would dearly like to be a master-craftsman, instead I am an employer of printers'.

Thus started a blissful period of life. It could have hardly have been otherwise, they were such delightful people to work with and for the first time I was actually allowed to be creative. I regard North Norfolk as halfway to heaven. We renovated an old farmhouse, which provided a happy base for our family who were coming and going – university, teacher training, growing up rapidly, getting married. It was a happy time all round. Too good to last. The speed of change in printing technology was rapid – too rapid if one lacked expertise and capital. After only seven years another change of direction was necessary, and that was when Mary and I moved to the Old Forge and embarked on a fascinating exercise in the world of antiques.

I have told the story of our happy days at the Old Forge in *A Living in the Past*, so let me tell you a little about the biggest restoration job we ever handled – Briggate House.

Living in a rented cottage, I had already started my new employment. At weekends we went on hilarious excursions, exploring North Norfolk and looking at a great number of properties offered for sale. I admit that for estate agents we were difficult customers. We didn't know what we wanted but knew we would recognise it when we saw it!

Then, one lunch-time, Mary and William, who was down from university, came to see me bubbling over with excitement. Could I come at once and see what they had found? We went off through Meeting House Hill, along the single track road with grass in the middle to Briggate, where they proudly showed me their find.

They had been cruising around and stopped at the T-junction to look at the map. 'That house looks empty,' said William, so they pulled on to the little triangular green in front of the house and had a walk round. It wasn't just empty, it was crying out for love and attention. There was no 'For Sale' notice, not even a name on the gate, so they found a neighbour, asked about it and then came to tell me the news. The neighbour had not been able to tell them much beyond the fact that it had been empty for a long time and belonged to a local farmer. We phoned and agreed to meet at the farmer's office - an impressive place giving sure indication that farming is a hi-tech industry, no longer based on empirical formulae and rule of thumb.

Yes, he said, he would consider selling the place. He had been half-expecting that one of his sons would want the place but that now seemed improbable. He would need to get a valuation and would be in touch. Yes, we were welcome to have a look round, and we would find the key up the spout of the lead pump in the yard behind the house.

Anyone in their right mind would have waited till next day. We were far too excited and drove straight there to continue our exploration. It was coming on for dusk when we got there. Perhaps the gentle light of the setting sun added a glow to the soft red bricks, failed to reveal the state of the pillared front entrance, enhanced the artistic grouping of the barn and other outbuildings while filtering out much of the dereliction. One way or the other it made no difference; we were hooked.

We found the key as instructed. It was six inches long and more suitable for a church door or a dungeon. It was, of course, for the back door – who (except Mary) would expect otherwise? Front doors in these parts being more for weddings and funerals than for daily use.

The last of the daylight showed through the roof in places and at least one floor moved ominously underfoot. There were sundry unpleasant smells, stale wood-smoke, mildew and damp sacking. Nothing put us off, we were enraptured.

Our next move was to get a Mr Norgate to come and have a look. He had been recommended to us by friends as the right man for the job, a man with a genuine feel for and an interest in old buildings, a practical builder who would be more enlightening than a conventional surveyor. He endeared himself to us by being just as enthusiastic as we were. His quiet gentle manner, sense of humour and shining optimism were much more than we had dared hope for.

While the legal formalities ground their way slowly towards completion of purchase (I have always suspected that the agreed price bore close relation to the price of a new combine harvester) we were given permission to move our caravan into the yard, so we gave up the rented house and moved in. It was frustrating seeing so much that we would have liked to have got on with and having to wait until we were the owners. We took the liberty of replacing about a hundred pantiles on the cartlodge and looseboxes, and noted that the tiles were underlaid with reeds between the battens – an early form of insulation. We used one of the looseboxes as an ablution, where we were watched by a pair of nesting swallows.

Then one day it was all ours. Mr Norgate's men arrived with commendable speed and made a good start on ripping out the more obvious portions of rot and making good the roof. The overall plan was that they would deal with all restructuring, would subcontract plumbing and electrification and we would do all the painting and decorating. The telephone engineers arrived. 'Where would you like the phone?' they asked. There was no obvious place, so half in jest Mary said, 'Better stick it on the wall'. It was an excellent solution, and one we have used in subsequent homes.

Mr Norgate was unflappable, nothing fazed him. 'Yes, Mrs Hill, we can stitch that wall together'. 'That damp is no problem. We will inject on the outside and treat the inside like a boat!' 'Certainly we can build a fireplace, using those bits you've found in the garden and some stimulated (sic) stone.'

One morning Mark and Alex, Mr Norgate's bright sparks, were scheduled to remove a partition to make one good-sized room of two rather meagre ones. Mary was writing letters in the caravan out in the yard. She heard a lot of laughter, a rending sort of crash and then a curious silence. After a lengthy pause Alex appeared.

'I think you'll be wanting a new ceiling in that room,' he offered.

'Why?' asked Mary, 'What's wrong with it?'

'Well, that sort of come down,' explained Alex, and a tour of inspection made clear that the old partition, crude though it had been, had actually been holding up the ceiling.

The result of that jollification was that the room that became William's was the only one in the house with a brand new plasterboard ceiling; the only ceiling without interesting undulations and certainly the only one totally devoid of the good old traditional horsehair content.

The pillared porticos proved to be a hollow mockery. The twin pillars at the front were made of wood plastered over, and the half-pillars on the wall disintegrated at a touch. Mr Norgate regarded dry rot as no more serious than inflamed tonsils or a decayed tooth. He also prescribed a new front door - actually a recycled one with genuine bottle-glass lights.

Living on site, Mary was able to act as sort of clerk of works, to oversee the alterations and to be consulted on any problematical matters, such as the plumber's quandary. He came and said that the only way that he could see to run the pipes for the upstairs radiators would be across the stairs.

'You box them in and carpet over.' Mary said, 'No. Think again.' He went away for a week, and came back with an acceptable solution. She was also on hand when a shoe was discovered under a floorboard beside a fireplace. We sent it to Norwich Museum, whence it was forwarded to Northampton, where a Miss Swann was writing a treatise on buried and hidden shoes. She dated it between 1730 and 1760. We decided to let the museum keep it on indefinite loan. We also uncovered some wallpaper which eventually reached the Victoria and Albert Museum. They confirmed that it was a hand-blocked paper, but we were a little disappointed that they dated it no earlier than mid-Victorian.

Much later, when we got around to painting, Mary discovered an inscription on the top edge of a door. Scratched in copperplate hand it read, 'Wm. Cook painted this June 23rd 1802'. How satisfying to think that our door had been painted three years before the Battle of Trafalgar. We were only mildly surprised to find that William Cook was buried in Worstead Churchyard at about the same date as that on the extension to our barn, which was added in 1840 by E.T., whoever he may have been.

William Cook's room, or the dining room as we came to call it, was the last one we tackled. We didn't really need a dining room. By that time the big farmhouse kitchen had become the centre of life. It was warm, had direct access to the cellar and had views to the courtyard and walled garden. Another discovery made by the 'Clerk of the Works' was that the banisters on the rather elegant stairway were made of mahogany. It took hours and hours of painstaking work to remove the many layers of paint, and the result was a triumph. Meanwhile I continued to expose and clear the ornamental plaster frieze round the landing. It struck us as being rather over-grand for such a relatively humble house. Mr Norgate suggested that it could have been executed by a plasterer taking lodgings at the farm while carrying out work in larger houses, and doing it as a gift or in part payment. The nymphs and satyrs and the portly character riding a donkey reminded me strongly of the cover illustrations on old copies of *Punch*.

All told, our first and biggest adventure in restoration took over a year. Other things were happening as well. Rosemary, our elder daughter, and husband Jon, produced our first grandson in West Africa. Fenella and Keith were married in that wonderful church in Worstead. William moved on from school to university and appeared from time to time. He was only marginally involved in the work of restoration, having other fish to fry such as organising an overland expedition to Turkey, walking the Pennine Way, sailing, shooting, and, one assumed, working for his degree.

Today, more than twenty years on, the situation is reversed. William runs his own show and I am only marginally involved, to the extent of one day each week, a day never without some good laughs and never without some interesting activities.

LOT 12
Caveat emptor

On one occasion William and I repaired a garden seat for a customer. All it needed was a couple of new slats in the back to replace broken ones. Easy enough to remove the old ones, that was accomplished in about thirty seconds. It took the best part of an hour to drill out the peg joints of the main frame to release the horizontals, to fashion two new teak slats and then reassemble the whole seat. We don't often work with teak. It is hard and durable, which makes it especially good for boat building, and it has the additional merit of not corroding iron, which is a great failing of oak.

I got the job of delivering the seat on my way home, New Buckenham being only a short way off my route. My maternal grandfather and great-grandfather were each in turn the village doctor there, so even a passing visit evokes memories of my mother's stories of people and events there before she married my father.

Mother was a great raconteur, almost obsessively interested in people and a splendid mimic. I recall one story about a friend of hers, a maiden lady called Harriet Munday. She was a well-known and much respected authority in the poultry world. The British Broadcasting Corporation wrote and asked if they might come and record an interview and discussion on poultry rearing.

Permission was granted, and on the appointed day an outside broadcasting van arrived and the engineers set up their recording equipment in one of the large hen-houses. This was long before television had been invented. The engineers soon found that the hen-house was not a good idea. The hens were so disturbed by the strange intrusion that they kept up a loud and continuous chorus of indignation. The sound was recorded and later used, at much reduced volume, as background noise.

The interview took place in the barn, and here the B.B.C. engineers met a second problem. They had expected Miss Munday to be what they imagined as a typical rural Norfolk female with a good regional accent; the whole thrust of the interview had been planned on this surmise. In fact, Miss Munday, though certainly of good Norfolk stock, was a very refined product of Felixstowe College and Girton, so a good deal of rethinking was required. The final programme, to which they all tuned in their wireless sets and listened some weeks later, was reckoned to be first rate. Of course Mother could produce all the accents and dialects for the story, just as she did when telling about the old gardener of theirs who saw no special merit in tidiness, yet always knew where things were to be found. He would issue instructions to the garden boy, such as: 'Them hoes 'ull be ahind the hen house', or 'That bucket 'ull be back of the privy,' or, my favourite, 'That scythe 'ull be up in the apple tree like it ollus is.'

Until I started going to auction sales I had forgotten the tale which Mother told about the one and only time she went to an auction on the cattle market at Bury St Edmund's. She was fascinated, as I have been, by the amazing speed and patter of the cattle auctioneer. She said that if you had ever thought or had the impression that rural folk were a bit slow in their mental processes, cattle sales would cause you to think again. As I found out at a much later date down in Sudbury, the deadstock sale often started before the livestock sale had finished. This made it very difficult to hear the auctioneer's voice above the loud protests of cattle being driven away to the station or loaded into floats. It was also necessary to watch where one put one's feet – a lesson in the meaning of 'to put one's foot in it'.

Mother said she had to screw up her courage to make a bid. The item which had caught her eye was a high-backed Windsor chair. She thought it would be absolutely right beside the kitchen range. Her heart was thumping as the auctioneer reached Lot 57.

'Now, ladies and gentlemen, here's a nice-looking chair... Who'll give me ten shillings for it?'

Ten shillings, thought Mother. That's a lot of money. Even so, she was just about to put up her hand when he continued, 'No takers at ten shillings? All right then, let's say five'.

She was sure that she went red in the face as she put up her hand, and was full of joy when to her delighted surprise the chair was knocked down to her. In her innocence she had not examined the chair, nor had she thought to question why it had been stood so firmly against the wall – its back legs were missing! Although she had to accept a fair measure of ridicule as she took home her two-legged chair, she was still quite pleased with it, and the village carpenter made a passable job of two new back legs.

Having learnt the meaning of *caveat emptor* at my mother's knee, I approached auction sales with caution, and I think that I probably went red in the face and wobbled a bit when bidding for our first house. Bidding in the sale room is just like gambling – you have to take a grip on yourself. There are always stories to be heard of wonderful finds and of being able to spot the swans that everybody else regarded as geese.

I actually knew someone who bought an inexpensive chest of drawers and found among the rubbish it contained a painting which he was able to sell for £300. That doesn't sound like a lot of money today – it seemed unbelievable at the time. There was another man who discovered an oil painting on the underside of a drawer in a mule-chest. Admittedly both men were dealers who knew what to look for. If I had not heard the story I could have lived to be a hundred without ever looking at the underside of a drawer – I now do so as a matter of course, but have yet to be rewarded.

The first auction I attended was that one where World's End, All Saints' Road, Pakefield came under the hammer. Later the name of the road was changed to Nightingale Road. This was doubly appropriate, as it joined Florence Road, and there were nightingales in the open space beside it, which later became a caravan site. The sale was not well attended, and the house failed to reach its reserve price and was withdrawn. I made an offer of one thousand five hundred pounds and it was ours. Between us Mary and I had five hundred, and raised a private mortgage for one thousand. It had to be a private mortgage, because the house stood so near to the erosion-prone cliff that building societies considered it a bad risk. Nearly sixty years on, the house still stands, and even more amazingly the beach has actually built up and new houses have been built even nearer to the cliff edge.

Even for such an insignificant sale, printed particulars had been produced. Mary has our copy stashed away somewhere. The item which I best remember is a charming description of the front garden, said to include 'a winding path between lawns', a truly romantic version of a concrete path with a kink in it. So this was not only my first experience of an auction but also an introduction to auctioneers' and estate agents' jargon, both of which have continued to fascinate me. I suggest that the definitive work on the latter is a small book by Norman Thelwell entitled *This Desirable Plot*.

I can't leave the subject without another quotation from those particulars: 'Pakefield is well known for its bracing and invigorating air'. If we didn't know that before we went to live there, we soon found out. In winter it was no uncommon thing to have sand and salt spray on our windows. During our first winter there the sea reached the foot of the cliff with each gale and a little more of Pakefield was lost. My father, who had been at school in Lowestoft, used to speak of there having been three fields on the seaward side of Pakefield Church. We saw only one house demolished on the cliff edge before new major sea defence works began to have effect. The sheet piling groynes and the Jubilee Parade helped to build up the level of the beach. In the '40s 'our' beach, between The Gap and Scull Gap, was still relatively unused. Certainly there were summer evenings when we needed to walk only a little way to be able to swim happily without swimsuits. But its popularity grew, so that, just as in 1812 'several excellent bathing machines were stationed on the beach', a handful of beach huts appeared below the church. The number of summer visitors grew each year as caravan sites proliferated, and the holiday camp took over again from the Italian P.O.W.s.

Although Pakefield had lost its identity as a fishing village, part having disappeared into the sea and the remainder being incorporated into the borough of Lowestoft as far back as 1934, it still retained some of its charm and community feeling. It was certainly a good place in which to bring up children. The beach in summer was a daily playground, and as they grew our games became more sophisticated; toy boats were replaced by the real thing, which we sailed off the shingle beach. On almost the last of such outings our youngest, William, with a friend who shortly became our son-in-law, had the misfortune to capsize. The rescue helicopter was alerted and was quickly on the scene, but they declined to be rescued and brought the boat ashore.

It was not long before we began to heave sighs of relief in the autumn when the visitors had all departed and the beach was ours again. This was the time when two or three longshore boats would return to the serious business of fishing. In our early days the fishing was not a highly organised affair. Lorry-loads of fish boxes and all the trappings of commercial activity came later. Joe Easty was a friend who sold us fish at nominal prices, or was just as likely to offer us a present of grilse or mackerel so fresh that the water was still dripping off them and their gills had hardly stopped moving. October herring and sprats were seasonal dishes to look forward to. There was some shrimping done on the bank a few yards off-shore, and it was there that another friend, Bob Evans, was stung by a weaver fish. He lay in agony in our drawing room waiting for the doctor, and declared that the pain would not ease until the tide turned. He was right!

As line-fishing from the beach became more popular, we suffered weekend invasions by the coach-load. We were happy that they too could enjoy our beach, though less pleased with the litter they left behind. On many a Sunday a rod and line, with or without large umbrella and hamper, could be seen every few yards all the way to the wreck and beyond to Kessingland. The wreck was a portion of an assault landing craft, reputedly washed up from the Normandy landings. It lay partly submerged in the sand below Crazy Mary's Hole. Each year abrasion wore the steel sheeting thinner, until it finally crumpled and disappeared.

As autumn gave way to winter we thought less highly of the beach. It became a cold, exposed place, to be visited less frequently. The north-east gales brought that salt spray and sand to our windows. It was always a source of disappointment that the tidal scour along the coast deprived us of driftwood. About two hundred yards of cliff path were lost on the night of the East Coast Floods in 1953. The rebuilt church was left uncomfortably near the edge. Two of our children had been christened there, and our elder daughter married. For us, her wedding marked the end of an era; we moved away two days later.

LOT 13
Difficult deliveries

I don't very often get called on to help make deliveries of purchases to customers' homes. When I do, it is almost always a large, heavy and potentially awkward piece of furniture. A typical example recently was a fairly massive oak dining table. I had already met this particular beast, it was one of a pair which William had bought and we had collected from a house over on the edge of Breckland. I remember that road with pleasure, because along there William collects animal feed, and on one occasion when I was with him he bought some bales of hay. As we loaded them into the van several chickens insisted on getting in as well, and had to be firmly ejected.

But that is beside the point. When we got around to dealing with the first of those tables, it was a beautiful sunny day and we were tempted to work outside. This proved to be a good move, especially when we reached the stage of wax polishing, as the warmth softened the wax, helping to produce a satisfactory finish. The weather nearly beat us. Just in time we saw a black cloud coming up. We heaved the table into the van and finished the job in there.

I didn't see that table again for a couple of weeks, during which time William had taken it to Risby Barn, and the next I heard it had been sold and could I help with delivery on Saturday? Yes! Of course I could, an outing with William is not to be missed, and Mary came too for the ride. Woolpit was our destination. Mary and I lived there briefly in our nomadic period. It has grown hugely in the last twenty years, but still looks to be a pleasant village, much enhanced by its bypass.

We found the cottage without difficulty, but that is where the difficulties began. In addition to that table we were also delivering a splendid (and heavy) seaman's chest and a very solid pine cupboard. William did a reconnaissance. From the van, things didn't look promising, but I had great faith, which was justified. The first two items went in through the front door with no more than two inches to spare. The chest had to be up-ended, turned 90 degrees and eased past the new paint into the sitting room. It sat in the room looking like Napoleon's tomb. The new owner was delighted with it, especially after we had moved it twice so that the hinges were away from the window and it was still possible to open the door.

The pine cupboard was even heavier, and a closer fit through the front door. It had to be manoeuvred around the foot of the stairs, turned on its axis 90 degrees to the right this time, and eased into the dining room. Someone asked if there was going to be room for it and the table. We supported the proposition that we should give it a try, as the alternative was to take the cupboard up the stairs – and we had already seen them!

The day was getting warmer as we lifted the table out of the van and started our circumnavigation of the cottage to reach the back door. To describe our progress sounds rather like a gymnastics class; legs down, legs up to the right, legs down. Legs up to the left, mind the bay tree, legs down, rest. We had arrived at the sun room, where we were faced with three doorways to be negotiated, with sharp turns to the dining room. I am not over-dramatising when I say that we got in not with inches to spare, but millimetres. I was content to see the last of that table, looking absolutely splendid in its new home, and only a little saddened thinking of its twin still to be disposed of.

'What's the trouble?' asked William this morning, solicitous as always concerning my welfare. I had to admit to a bruised hip, having fallen out of a skip the previous evening. Of course I ought to know better at my time of life and not climb into skips, but I had been unable to resist the lure of a sizeable oak beam which lay in the bottom. It had proved heavier and more awkward than I had anticipated. An empty skip is at all times difficult to climb in or out of. It is more usual to encounter skips which have been filled, and indeed it is almost a rarity to find one that has not been over-filled.

Chambers' Concise Dictionary, my infallible source of information, defines a skip as 'A box or trunk for raising minerals from a mine; a large container for transporting building materials etc., theatrical costumes or refuse'. I am enchanted at the thought of finding theatrical costumes. Over the years we have salvaged a wide variety of objects but never yet anything so exotic. My sister-in-law used to live in Islington, where she met a strange reversal of taking things from skips. She had one delivered prior to doing some alterations and clearing garden rubbish. She found that neighbours took advantage of the opportunity to do a little dumping, and the skip was half full before she even started her own disposals.

The largest item we have rescued was a mahogany shop counter. We chanced to be passing at the moment it was being dumped, and took it away with the blessing of the disposer. Treasures on a more modest scale have included framed pictures, maple frames, a mahogany loo seat, assorted chairs and a perfectly usable bicycle. In my semi-retirement I have not lost interest in the contents of skips; the focus of my attention has moved on to timber, and the debris and off-cuts from building operations have filled my woodshed and kept my wood-burning stove well supplied. The exercise which I get at my saw-horse reminds me of the saying 'He who cuts his own wood is twice warmed'.

But getting back to the subject of difficult deliveries, I recall witnessing one of the most difficult and neatly executed deliveries I'd seen in a long time, when William and I were assisting at a house clearance in Mildenhall.

Reconnaissance had shown that a skip would be needed and had also revealed that the only place for it to stand was in the narrow opening at the side of the house. We would not have been popular with it standing in the narrow street. The skip operator made what we saw as a difficult delivery look easy. With no hesitation beyond a quick look up the alleyway, he backed in, lowered the skip with inches to spare, and was away in moments. There was no possibility of our using the side door of the house; everything had to come out through the front.

There was some sort of rough justice in the fact that when Mary and I moved into Corner Cottage it quickly became clear that when it was built in about 1850 no one visualized the furniture or domestic appliances of the future. Our penchant for D.I.Y has always included doing our own furniture removals with a hired van. Even with the experiences of six moves we were not prepared for the difficulties of inserting some of our larger pieces into the cottage. Even William was not able to persuade a single divan bed up the steep little staircase. We had to remove a bedroom window and pass it in from the top of the van. Happily, our two large chests of drawers had met this situation years before they came into our possession, and had been beautifully cut in half. The large pine cupboard destined for what would become the bathroom had to be taken to pieces and rebuilt in situ. The new bath for that room had an awkward trip in through the back door, along the passage, round the corner and just, but only just, up those stairs. Prudently I held myself aloof from that operation. It was definitely a difficult delivery and I make no claim to be a plumber.

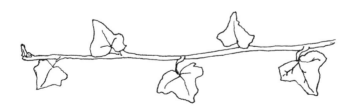

LOT 14
Muck and money

A good many years ago an itinerant thief broke into our laundry premises at Lowestoft and stole a clean change of clothing. The worst mistake he made was stealing clothes that belonged to a policeman. I am sure this added impetus to his pursuit and apprehension. The local newspaper ran the story under the headline, 'Grime Doesn't Pay.' The reporter was a friend of mine, always glad of a good story, and I had no doubt that a story was worth much more than paid advertising.

The reason I mention this is that I have come home filthy today after time in the workshop with William. I am hopeful that if grime doesn't pay, it will on the other hand be true that where there's muck there's money.

Dealing with antiques, especially in the area of furniture repair and restoration, is not all artistic and aesthetic work, there is often an element of near-drudgery and generous helpings of filth. The nadir is reached with the abysmal matter of 'stripping.' While one may lament the huge quantities of good pine furniture that has been painted, I suppose that one ought also to acknowledge that in many cases the paint has preserved the item. Nevertheless, removing layers of paint is an unpleasant business. I almost said 'ancient layers of paint', which would have been an error, for modern paint is even more difficult than earlier kinds.

When we first came to this stripping chore we performed in one end of our barn. Working over an old bath, we sprinkled caustic soda crystals into a plastic bucket containing a couple of pints of boiling water and quickly scrubbed the article on which we were working. The nauseous sludge produced could be rinsed off with more hot water, and if necessary the procedure repeated. After rinsing, the wood was wiped down, and, to neutralise any remaining traces of caustic, was wiped over with a diluted solution of vinegar. Plenty of fresh air and sunshine was desired for drying. It is always a mistake to allow the moisture to soak into the wood. We christened this part of the process 'Son and Heir'.

Of course I ought to have mentioned protective clothing. Caustic burns on skin are unpleasantly painful, and exceedingly dangerous in eyes. So the prudent stripper, far from dancing provocatively on stage and removing garments, will put on a hat, goggles, full length plastic apron, rubber boots and elbow-length plastic gloves, and still work with caution, remembering that the scrubbing brush can easily flick spray in one's face.

This sort of procedure works well for small items, anything, say, up to the size of a chair. Beyond that, it becomes necessary to find a stripper with a tank, and preferably a hot tank, which reduces the period of immersion necessary and thereby avoids the wood becoming sodden. A cold tank can be just as effective so long as each job is watched carefully to avoid over-long immersion.

Hot or cold immersion is best followed by thorough rinsing with a pressure washer, a quick wipe down and speedy drying. A look at the local weather forecast is a good idea before starting the entertainment.

Life has moved on since we started stripping. At that date Nitromors stripper was available, a highly toxic and unpleasant chemical paint-remover and, of course, relatively much more expensive. There are, however, cases where it is unwise to use caustic. Mahogany and sometimes oak is liable to turn black if treated with caustic, and some modern paints can only be removed satisfactorily with specially designed removers, of which there is now a choice on the market.

Stripping is not only achieved by chemical means; sheer hard work with scrapers and sanders is sometimes possible, or even preferable. Both rotary and reciprocating sanders need to be handled with care, and alone will never produce the fine finish of dedicated hand-working with graded sandpaper and steel wool. At which point I must again mention protective clothing. Steel wool breaks down to very fine particles which give rise to excruciating pain if embedded in the skin, especially in the soles of one's feet! So, suitable gloves, overalls and boots are sensible, even if they appear disproportionate.

I've written elsewhere about mud at farm sales, and the filth that is sometimes encountered in house clearances. The insect and animal world is sometimes an unexpected hazard. Infestation by wood beetles is something one looks for and tries to avoid. It can be effectively treated, but no one entirely trusts a piece of furniture which shows signs of earlier beetle activity. Moths, butterflies, beetles, spiders and mice regularly turn up in furniture. It is almost a tradition to find a mouse-hole at the back of a corner cupboard.

On one occasion we bought a butcher's block which produced a surprise. Wonderful creations, those composite butcher's blocks. After extended use they have usually been turned over so that one, if not both sides, has been worn away to resemble a relief map of rolling downland. We scrubbed the block, and planned to oil it when dry. Then we gave our attention to the very substantial base. It looked to be well scrubbed and needing little work. By chance we turned it on one side and happened to look at the bottoms of the legs – they were each cavities, alive with very healthy maggots! A fair number of butcher's blocks came on the market after E.U. regulations banned them from butchers' shops.

The latest insanity from Brussels has been the proposal that all sheep's horns must be classified as 'specific risk material' or be incinerated. This is because, some time back, British scientists suggested that sheep might catch Mad Cow Disease. They admitted that no sheep had actually caught it, but as 'a precautionary principle' it was decided in Brussels that all sheep's heads should be destroyed, and that this should include the horns. What, you may ask, has this to do with art and antiques? The answer is that sheep's horns are used for the carving of stick handles, and have been so used for generations. There is indeed a Stick Dressers' Association. Much of the work of stick dressers is very beautiful indeed, and is fully appreciated by no less than Her Majesty the Queen and Prince Charles.

Those beautiful, ornately carved stick handles have much in common with shepherds' crooks and bishops' crosiers. The crooks that pass through our workshop are customarily workaday examples but even they are beautiful in their simplicity. An article which has evolved through use over thousands of years is deeply evocative.

I have strayed (like a lost sheep?) from my theme of muck and money, to which I may return by way of cromes, dydles, drainage tools and even a mention of the small building down the garden path.

The first family four-holer I encountered was at Hollybush Farm. In the traditional manner of farmers' wives, Aunt Cissy managed a flock of hens. The hen-house was between the kitchen door and the orchard, and the privy stood just beyond it. In the orchard there were usually half a dozen geese, who kept the grass down and gorged themselves on windfall apples. A tranquil scene, you might think, and so it was until someone walked down the path to the privy. The chickens would come running and squawking in anticipation of a feed, the geese would shriek and often as not come towards one with necks outstretched in a threatening manner – a modest and unobtrusive visit was impossible.

The little building itself was of brick construction with a Welsh slate roof. A large elderberry bush overshadowed one end and a rampant rose decorated the other. Behind was a dense nettle bed, alive with butterflies. I cannot now remember what colour the door was painted, probably a good serviceable agricultural green. There were no windows. The only source of light and ventilation when the door was closed was a cut-out star of David. The idea of maintaining a gloomy interior was to discourage flies. It is more usual to find a cut-out triangle or a serrated top to the door, but these are facts which I was to learn in later years. Much later, in fact, for it was fully forty years before I became the owner of a privy and began to take an interest in such important matters.

Mary and I had moved from a relatively urban area on the Suffolk coast to the wilds of North Norfolk. The mod. cons. in our farmhouse were sketchy. True, there was a bath, a rusty Edwardian cast iron example on traditional ball and claw feet (one missing) set in the lower corner of an upstairs room. The plumbing put one in mind of Heath Robinson, or bagpipes. Cold water reached it by way of a lead-lined cistern in the roof and tepid water arrived fitfully from a vast black range in the kitchen. We never discovered the final destination of the waste water – a lead pipe disappeared beneath the cart-shed.

The privy was the nearest of three semi-detached outbuildings which formed one side of the enclosed backyard. Sad to relate, it was not a classic four, only a simple two-holer. Perhaps its only claim to fame was its outstanding cleanliness – whitewashed walls, well-scrubbed woodwork and pristine permanent floor. There was no fitting for toilet rolls, just a beautifully made wooden box for containing squares of paper, probably cut from the *Eastern Daily Press*. A small corner shelf supported a small blue and white enamel candle-holder and an Oxo tin for the box of matches. The only daylight came through three circular holes in the door – an imaginative effort compared with Holly Bush Farm.

We made no modifications to that paragon of a privy, and it served us well for the twelve months it took us to revamp the farmhouse into a des. res. Three moves later found us back in Suffolk. Corner Cottage was once the home of the village policeman, and probably pre-dated the introduction of the penny post. Despite a mantle of Clematis Montana Rubens, the little building in the yard immediately proclaims its original purpose. The serrated top to the door provides confirmation. Disappointment awaits inside, for it was long since dethroned and used as a coal-shed, probably about 1959 when main drains were installed in the village. Currently it serves as a tool shed and a totally inadequate workshop.

A small coincidence occurred this morning. I woke to frost patterns on the window and a chill east wind blowing outside. My thoughts went straight to that bleak, cold hotel building in Dunbar, where I was billeted briefly at the end of 1944. The loos were furnished with massive mahogany thrones with heavy brass fittings and blue and white willow-patterned bowls. They were so robustly proportioned that one might have thought them to be Georgian, though they must have been Victorian, contemporaneous with the building and owing much to the eponymous Mr Crapper. As I walked into the workshop the first things I saw were a pair of mahogany loo seats. Cleaning and polishing them was my first job of the day.

What marvellous wood mahogany is! We don't handle or work with mahogany very often, it's not our style, but when the chance arises it gives us real pleasure. In colour and texture it is so different from the softwoods and English hardwoods with which we usually work. I don't know it well enough to be able to distinguish between the American, Philippine and African varieties. I do, on the other hand, remember walking through a stand of teak in Nigeria. The ground was deeply covered with large fallen leaves and gave the impression of being dry. In fact the lower layers of leaves held water as might a layer of soup plates, so that I was soon wet almost to my knees.

One of the more interesting pieces of carved mahogany which we have handled was an elaborate Purdonium. You will know that Mr Purdon was a nineteenth century inventor who designed and gave his name to a kind of coal scuttle with a hinged sloping front and a coal shovel slotted into a bracket at the back. It was intended to reduce the dust caused by shovelling coal onto the fire. From utilitarian origins, many elaborate examples were produced, some even appearing in the Chippendale catalogue.

Well, the one of which I am telling came from my son-in-law John. I had collected it from Chalfont St Peter and was driving home through London with the splendid article in the back of our estate car. I drew up at traffic lights and another car drew up beside me.

'What in the world have you got there?' asked the other driver.

'A Purdonium,' I shouted as the lights changed and we all moved forward to the next set of lights.

'What's a Purdonium?' he asked, and I gave a short description as the lights turned gr een. At the next set we were somewhere near Madame Tussaud's. 'Is it for sale?' was the next question, and I have to spoil what could have been a good story by recording that traffic conditions separated us, so that I failed to make a quick sale.

Napthalene (mothballs) help to preserve fur of stuffed animals.

Oriental furniture – the more elaborate the better.

Panama hats can be cleaned with white bread.

Quick fix for tortoiseshell – rub with almond oil.

Repair papier mâché with Polyfilla; smooth down and paint.

Steel wool – available in various grades, invaluable for producing a good surface on wood.

LOT 15
Bric-a-brac

My dictionary informs me that 'bric-a-brac' means miscellaneous small objects, especially furniture and curios, kept because they are ornamental or rare. More interestingly, it also gives the derivation as being from the French *'de bric et de brac'* which can be translated as 'by hook or by crook'. All of which leaves the field wide open, and one would be hard pressed to disqualify almost anything seen on a bric-a-brac stall so long as it was small.

Many a memento clearly falls into the bric-a-brac category. I have a fifty-piastre piece, which was missing for many years and then found again, lying snugly in the bottom of my round leather stud box. I find it hard to think that I would ever need or want to be reminded of my time in Egypt. I have remarkably vivid memories of the sand of the desert, the waters of the Nile, the hump of the camel and the Sphinx's inscrutable smile. Images of Cairo and Alexandria are less sharp, but I passed through the canal three times – it felt like a living history and geography lesson, and the Bitter Lakes were truly beautiful. If having gone through the canal three times makes it sound as if I now ought to be somewhere beyond the far end, the discrepancy arises by having gone round the Cape of Good Hope the first time out.

The fact is one collects bric-a-brac without even trying. On the mantelpiece at home there are two brass tortoises. We had one in which we kept postage stamps; someone saw it, and, as in the case of the friend who inadvertently collected frogs, assumed that we liked tortoises and gave us its twin. That really started the rot, and I now count six brass reptiles lurking among the two brass candlesticks, one antique and one repro, an ashtray, a bowl, a World War 1 matchbox case and the carriage clock. Given a free hand I would retain only the latter, and would make a considerable saving on Brasso.

We lived in the parish of Long Melford for several years, yet until today I had never heard of a 'Long Melford' and had certainly not seen one. Our lunch companion at the White Horse produced one from his pocket. We had been saying how quickly keys and coins wear a hole in one's pocket. 'Here you are,' he said, 'the perfect answer to the problem, a Long Melford.' A simple answer too; it was a plain soft leather bag, rectangular, about eight inches long and three and a half wide. The size is critical, as one must be able to get one's hand into it and yet it must not be too big to fit snugly into one's pocket.

Unfortunately, Ronnie could not throw any light on the origin of the name. One can only assume that it derives from its place of origin. I can readily picture George Borrow producing such an article when making a

55

payment at one of the horse fairs which he attended in that village. But that is quite fanciful and I would welcome enlightenment.

The little cobblestone cottage in Blakeney where Mary and I are staying at the moment offers another example of inadvertent collecting. I find it hard to believe that the owner would have intentionally amassed such a plethora of bric-a-brac. My impression is that transient visitors such as ourselves have added to the décor. A basket-work dish on the pine dresser offers a fascinating collection of seashells which asks to be added to. The mantelpiece, over a very serious-looking wood-burning stove, carries two pottery cottages waiting to develop into a street, a model boat and three seals waiting to be fed, one wooden, one ceramic and one soapstone. Tomorrow, depending on the weather, we will go out to the Point and see the real thing. Also on the dresser are five dried flower creations, ten assorted plates and jugs, a whimsy mouse, a frog playing a violin and a mole emerging from a stylised flowerpot. We will have to search diligently if we wish to make an original addition.

The 'small furniture' mentioned in the dictionary definition of bric-a-brac is slightly puzzling to me. How small is small? Stools, perhaps, and one might include cutlery boxes, caddies, wine coolers and even odd items such as apothecaries' chests or pole-screens, though I would hardly call them furniture – some would come within the classification of 'objects of virtu'. If one insists on classifying, then there are still baubles, bibelots, curios, gewgaws, knick-knacks, ornaments and trinkets – something for everyone.

But how, I ask myself, would one classify Tilley lamps? It's a long time since I last heard the sound of a pump followed by the distinctive 'plop' as the vaporised fuel exploded into light and the mantle changed from dead white to an incandescent glow. A pleasant warm light, it had only one disadvantage, and that was the way it attracted insects in from the surrounding darkness.

I associate these lamps with tented encampments or palm-thatched *bashas* in far-flung corners of the British Empire; in particular, corners into which I have been flung, such as the banks of the river Ogun in West Africa or the arid wastes of Karvetnagar, inland from Madras. Now I note to my surprise that anglers still use Tilley lamps beside the Swangey lakes, only a few yards from Ford Farm, where I go every week. So Tilley lamps, like me, have outlived the British Empire.

My other indelible and associated memory is of an evening many years ago when I was out on another campaign trail, this time not military but political. 'Go to Henstead,' I was directed, 'and hold the fort until the candidate arrives.' Henstead is more of a lovely idea than a place, in a gentle green valley where the Hundred river itself is so placid that it never actually exerts itself to reach the sea, simply dissipating itself in lush meadows and a no man's land of sand, shingle and coarse grass. I arrived in profound darkness, parked in the playground, negotiated what seemed to be a monsoon drain, and followed the sound of voices into the building. Someone was trying to get a Tilley lamp to work. Suddenly it burst into flame and puffed gently before spreading its glow of warm light. After a short tussle it was joined by a second lamp, and the school room took shape around us. A faint whiff of paraffin was added to the standard scent of wax polish, chalk dust and well-used gym shoes.

'Well', said the lamp-lighter, 'that's better, now we can get some chairs in from the other room.' As was to be expected, none of the chairs proved to be large enough for adult use. We carried them in and set them in order. More people arrived. I would not have been surprised if I had been told that they were the entire adult population of Henstead. At least we would have had a choice if picking a football team. The lamp-lighter identified himself as chairman of the meeting. 'We ought to have a speaker to fill in until the candidate arrives,' he announced. 'That's right,' I said. We shook hands and introduced ourselves; I was introduced to the audience and was up on my feet.

I glanced at the clock, 7.50. The candidate was due at 8 o'clock. I had been prepared to speak for half an hour, so this should be easy, cut out all the padding, I told myself, and get right down to the bones of the matter. I don't now recall what the matter was; probably the ill-conceived groundnut scheme, the chicken-farming fiasco in the Gambia or some such ineptitude. Eight o'clock, and I had come to an end. No candidate in sight. I hadn't planned to invite questions but could see no other course. They were kind to me. I could talk about Nigeria from personal experience but was getting a bit thin on that by 8.15. Then mercifully the door opened and, 'Mr Chairman, ladies and gentlemen, here is our candidate – Jim Prior'. I had been properly briefed by the Agent, Donald Millar. 'When the candidate arrives, you fade.' I faded promptly and thankfully.

No doubt the memory of that occasion remains so clear because it was the subject of the first article I wrote for the *Eastern Daily Press*. It was the beginning of an association which continued for nearly twenty years, during most of which time I was getting an article accepted once each month, until a new broom swept away the slot for which freelance contributions were accepted. I was sad when that gentle activity came to an end, as it had always stimulated me to be aware of my surroundings and to be constantly on the lookout for a subject of interest.

LOT 16
Golf is only a game

Mary and I often go to the White Horse for lunch on Tuesdays. While there recently I heard a noise which I had not registered for some long time. Looking round the end of the high-backed settle I saw a game of dominoes in progress, accompanied by that characteristic click of the tiles on a wooden tabletop.

Certainly we have handled sets of dominoes over the years, but I have always regarded them as works of art, which many of them are, or simply as stock-in-trade bygones. I realise that I can't actually remember when I last played the game.

Sporting memorabilia is not an area into which we have done much more than dip our toes. It is one of the many areas best left to the specialists, and for the same reason we have never done more than dabble in such fields as silver and china, or clocks and watches. All of these things have passed through our hands from time to time, especially in the case of house clearances, but we have never sought them.

I was thinking that I had a personal blind spot as far as sporting memorabilia is concerned, but I note that I still have my '30' cap. It is a sort of skullcap with a tassel on top and a symbolic eagle badge, awarded, if I remember correctly, to individuals in the second and third fifteens (at least that would seem to make the arithmetic right.) I can't imagine when or even if we ever wore them.

First XV colours were not awarded automatically, they were dished out to individual players as the season progressed. This gave me one of my worst moments. It was the regular practice for the school to assemble in the hall (Big School) on Fridays instead of going into Chapel. This gave the headmaster an opportunity to make pronouncements, and he was followed by the Head Boy, who among other things would announce the award of colours. I was, as they say, sweating on the top line and tolerably sure that my name would be read out, so when he read out, 'First Fifteen colours for 1937 are awarded to D.G...' I was halfway up on my feet, only to sit down again, red in the face, when he concluded, '....Farquar.' D.G.Hill had to agonise for another week. When the *Sunday Times* reported our match with K.C.S. Wimbledon and noted, 'The Epsom hooking was so good that they got the ball back nearly every time,' I felt that I had made the grade, and was not disappointed the following Friday.

Those caps were much more elaborate creations. I note that we did not wear them even for the team photograph. They were definitely a relic from times of former glory, and must now be collectable.

It is obvious that I am in a minority in this matter as the appetite for sporting memorabilia is huge, perhaps fanatical is a better word, and the range of material for avid collectors is endless, ranging from cigarette cards of famous sportsmen to sweaty shirts from the backs of Wimbledon stars, and Man U's 19th strip, and now I see that England caps fetch enormous sums.

When I mentioned this to William he pointed out that we have not been quite as 'unsporting' as I made out, because over the years a range of equipment and gear from sporting days of the past have passed through our hands, and of them all the most truly antique have been pub games. An early example he remembered was a shove ha'penny board which Mary found blocking up a hole in the corner of a barn. Mary has always excelled at spotting unconsidered trifles in unexpected places. We have handled several pairs of 'woods', usually in well-constructed leather holders. Bowls strike me as rare examples of truly beautiful sports equipment. The lignum vitae of which they are usually made is itself a rare beauty among woods, where the competition is stiff.

I may be courting displeasure by including bowls in my review of pub games. Apart from archery, it is supposed to be the most ancient of British games. Greens have traditionally been associated with public houses. Public authorities and clubs have greatly upgraded the image of the game, and from observation I would say that few sports or games offer a higher standard of sartorial turnout. (That should ease me back into favour.)

The image of croquet is rather less secure. The game has a much shorter pedigree, being of foreign extraction not much more than 150 years ago. It may well conjure up visions of sedate country house parties, ladies in crinolines and of immaculate green lawns, but my information is that it can be a vicious contest rather than a gentle summer afternoon's occupation. My sources of information have been my grandmother, who played for the county, and son-in law Jon, who played for Balliol. A good boxed set of equipment is a valuable item not to be passed over lightly at auction. Now I think about it, croquet can hardly be classed as a pub game, and having strayed from the point, I may as well mention that I was once foolish enough to say to my sister, 'Well, golf is only a game.'

'What do you mean, only a game?' she rounded on me, and I was lucky not to be clubbed. It is my simple view that the trouble with nearly all games is that people take them too seriously, so that they develop into gladiatorial contests, leaving no room for fun and uncomplicated pleasure.

An item of sports equipment that turns up from time to time is a set of metal quoits. I had always imagined that quoits would be a simple game, just a matter of getting one's quoit over the little peg set in its square of clay. Now I have been properly briefed and am duly amazed by the lore, language and tactics of the game, and the fact that its origins are lost in antiquity.

As in ancient crafts, this game has spawned a euphonious lexicon. The slightly convex side of the quoit is called the hill, the concave the hole. It may land in the clay hill-up, hole-up or stuck-up. The peg will probably be called the hob, and as with most of the terms there are regional variations. Then, when one starts to play, there are ringers, front-touchers, gaters, hillway, Q quoit and even Frenchmen to contend with. Even the dramatis personae have names; there is a bibber, a shower-up man and a trigman. But at this point I admitted defeat and retired confused to the bar.

There I learned that there is a National Quoits Association. A pity really, as it can only be a matter of time before Quoits features in the Olympic Games, thereby becoming transformed from a pleasant occupation enjoyed with a pint or two of beer, to a minor industry with sponsorship and drug-testing.

There are two pub games about which I have heard stories but have not yet seen: the Isle of Purbeck shove ha'penny board, and the Norfolk dart board. I am searching diligently for a Norfolk dart board, though I feel I may be about thirty years too late. The fact that our present targets are called dart boards confirms the idea that they were originally made of wood. The 'Norfolk' is reputed to have been made of elm, cut from a log of about 10 inches diameter, so that one would have been throwing into the end grain. The scoring area was only about six inches in diameter, and consisted of a Bull, Inner and Magpie which were worth 4, 3 and 1 points; the outer area scored no points. The usual game, they tell me, was 31 up, and as with most pub games there were local variations (no pun intended).

We had a customer at the Old Forge who was an interior designer. He was not a happy man; at the time he was working for one of the big brewers, and found the process of updating their pubs very mundane and depressing. As he put it, 'This life ain't all beer and skittles.' Well, skittles is another game with about as many variations as there are counties.

The talk in the sale room this week was about the set of golf clubs that had been sold last week. The story emerging was that those clubs had been left at the dump with some other household rubbish. The attendant had prudently saved them, but had less prudently sold them for five pounds. The new owner had offered them to a third party for fifty pounds. His offer had been rejected, so he put them in the auction sale and, as we all knew, they had been knocked down for fifteen hundred pounds. It had been one of those rare moments when the room fell silent. If you are lucky enough to be interested in the next lot, this is a good moment to jump in quickly before the general air of shock wears off, and achieve a successful maiden bid.

Tools should be cared for as a soldier cares for his rifle.

Uneven legs kill any furniture. Build up the short one in preference to shortening the others.

Varnish – old varnish can often be removed with turpentine.

Wax – a huge range of waxes is available to suit all requirements.

LOT 17
Another rush job

This week Mary and I went to a charity luncheon at Riddlesworth Hall (Princess Diana's school). We had a splendid meal in the equally magnificent surroundings and then went over to the assembly hall. The guest speaker was David Batty of Antiques Roadshow fame. He gave a charming light-hearted talk, mainly about his career in the world of antiques, from humble book porter to international celebrity.

In front of him on the platform he had a large table well stocked with artefacts which we, the audience, had brought for his appraisal. Wisely, but from our viewpoint sadly, he concentrated on oriental objects, these being his preferred specialisation. Mary and I had brought along one of a pair of huge blue and white dishes which we hoped he would identify and evaluate. He never got to it; now it is back on the wall with its partner and we still know little about the pair, although I have seen them hanging about all my life as they were one of my parents' wedding presents.

I picked up a couple of old crocks at the weekend. There is no need for laughter, I really mean two earthenware storage jars. They are big ones, just like the ones I remember standing in the pantry when I was a boy. One of these was used as a bread bin with a wooden bread board exactly fitting it as a lid. The other was filled with water-glass for preserving eggs. We kept chickens, and at times when they were laying well, eggs were preserved for when they went off the lay.

I am fairly sure that one of those I have just bought has also been used for preserving eggs. Silicate of soda, the main ingredient in what we called water-glass, leaves a deposit on the crock which I have never been able to remove. I have been told that one method is to bury the crock and leave it in the earth for several months – I've never tried this.

The street fair at Woolpit, where I found these two treasures, is a splendid affair. Like any outdoor event, it relies heavily on the weather for its success. This year it took place in blazing sunshine, and attracted a huge crowd. The village is closed to all traffic, cars are diverted to a field where stewards line them up with military precision. All along the main street and around the delightful village pump, stalls are set out from which almost anything you can think of is offered for sale – some would be very hard to think of. There is music, and an appetising smell of cooking in the air. There are games and competitions, a fancy-dress parade, and, as they say, all the fun of the fair.

Even at other times I enjoy Woolpit. Mary and I once parked our caravan alongside the site of the old pit from which the clay was dug for the production of rather unusual bricks – Woolpit Whites – more aesthetically pleasing than the ordinary run of rather yellow Suffolks. We enjoyed the church, which has exceptionally fine woodcarvings. In the Swan we learned the legend of the two green children, and various versions of the origin of the name Woolpit.

The festive air of the street fair and the impression that nearly all the residents of the village were taking an active part in the proceedings was reminiscent of the Worstead Village Festival. Now it is 25 years since we were involved in that event. Then it was already in its tenth anniversary year, and had grown into an enormous organisation from its simple beginnings as a flower festival in the church. The proceeds went to support the church restoration fund. I imagine that restoration work has long since been completed and that other projects now benefit.

Mary spent hot hours baking and steamy afternoons serving teas with members of the Women's Institute. I seem to recall doing a lot of washing-up. One year I went on show myself, and saw little of the rest of the activities. My sphere of action was in the barn at Holly Grove, which I shared with the Edgefield potters, a display of horse-brasses and a galaxy of glass bottles (all empty). Although the barn was more or less a backwater from the mainstream events, we had over a thousand visitors on the first day, and more on the other two. There were not many dull moments. I tried to make a tape recording, but the general hubbub and the potter's wheel thumping away in the background was all too much for the machine. By the end of the third day I had answered so many questions and been through my spiel so many times that I began to feel like a recording myself.

'Well no, this is not a commode, it's a prie-dieu. The lift-up top seat is for sitting on and the lower level is for kneeling on. As you can see, I have already rushed the seat and am now working on the kneeler... It is an interesting rather than a beautiful piece of furniture, probably not more than seventy or eighty years old. I have never handled another one quite like it. I have seen an illustration of one in Edwin Skull's catalogue dated 1852...The sad thing is that I am not able to get Norfolk rushes. There just aren't any to be found, and that is rather amazing when there used to be acres and acres of them. I've searched pretty thoroughly and the only ones I've found growing are a small group in Barton Broad. There are still some harvested in Bedfordshire and Huntingdon, and I have harvested some on the Suffolk/ Essex border...

Our rushes are so much better than those imported from Holland, Portugal and Poland. Ours are much more pliable, and mature to a beautiful range of colours...Many people confuse reeds and rushes. There are still large areas of reeds grown and harvested for thatching. One of the best places to see them growing or

being harvested is at How Hill, near Ludham... A reed is hollow, like a straw. No amount of dampening will soften it, which is what makes it so good for roofing...

Rushes are fibrous inside and soak up moisture. They grow right in the water, not on marshy ground like reeds. They are annual, ready for harvesting about June. After cutting they are dried and usually tied into "bolts" of about five pounds' weight and then can be stored indefinitely... It takes a day or so to damp them down to be ready for use. I have found the best way to do this is to wrap them in an old hop sack soaked in water, and then if possible leave them out in the rain...

Our local rushes have had various enemies including pollution, coypus, motor cruisers and general neglect. At the price we now pay for imported rushes it must soon become a paying proposition to cultivate them...

No, I don't do this full time. I accept only a small number of commissions... There is not a great deal to learn. I went to evening classes, but once one has learned the basics it becomes a matter of practice. Every chair seems to be slightly different, but there is only one basic pattern of rush-work which has to be adapted to the individual chair... On this chair I am twisting two rushes together all the time, trying to keep the thickness of the "rope" even and fairly light, in keeping with the style of the chair. A more robust chair can carry a correspondingly heavier seat, so might need three or even four rushes twisted into the rope... All the butt ends and joins are kept to the underside. From time to time I turn the chair over and have a tidy up, tucking in the stray bits and trimming the butts. I also introduce some stuffing into the pockets which are formed in the corners. The stuffing, which is all the odd bits and pieces of rush, tightens the work and gives the seat some fullness and shape...

When cutting away an old seat it is quite usual to find all sorts of material used for stuffing: sedge, hay or even paper. I have found straw which had evidently come straight from a chicken shed.'

Worstead's links with the past are represented by demonstrations of spinning and weaving in the church, and there are usually sheep too, being useful keeping down the grass in the churchyard.

They were golden days at Worstead. We loved our old farmhouse with its more than adequate barn, outbuildings and walled garden. The sadness was that we got there rather too late, Rosemary already married and out in West Africa, Fenella working as a designer for Pearsons of Chesterfield, and William at Reading University. Mary and I began to rattle around a bit. Briggate House would have made a splendid base for an antiques enterprise – except that it was not in the right place. Transplanted to somewhere near Long Melford, it could have been quite another matter.

LOT 18
Cobbles

As I came away from the dinghy park it suddenly struck me that I had seen only one wooden boat, an original style Enterprise, exactly the same as we used to sail from the beach at Pakefield some twenty-five years ago.

We tend to think nostalgically of old trades and crafts which have all but disappeared; we give rather less thought to new trades and technologies which in many cases have taken over from the old. Construction of boats in modern fibres and materials took over from wood with amazing speed, and although I am completely ignorant concerning the processes, they must surely by now have reached a point of such expertise that they can be ranked as a craft as much as an industrial process. (The double meaning of the word craft is causing me trouble.)

It pleases me to note as I walk along the quay and out along the hard that wood has not been totally excluded from the construction of many of the small boats, and still has a place in large and luxurious yachts. You don't have to be an old codger to appreciate the appearance of wood and its relative warmth compared with the corpse-like chill of plastic.

The first boat we owned at Pakefield was an early model 14-foot International, a beautiful boat, one to love, and on which endless hours of cosseting and work were needed. Each Spring found us struggling to get the boat ready in time for the Easter holidays. The weather was so often against us. Perhaps you have been involved in the Lowestoft Hockey Festival, which took place at Easter and was often, so it seemed, hailed by wisps of snow and a bitter north-east wind.

One year we were offered boathouse space in which to work. We thought that would take the sting out of our preparations, but there was another hazard: John, our benefactor, was a perfectionist and every time we felt we had finished he would say, 'Come on, now, one more coat of varnish.' The Enterprise which followed was much easier to maintain. I never had any love for marine plywood, but she was a good family boat which we could trail anywhere and slip in, here at Blakeney or at places such as Lake Lothing, or anywhere around the Norfolk Broads.

When the crew had all left home, I moved down the scale to a Heron; a rather infantile boat which I could manage on and off its trailer single-handed. And then, like the old sailor who walked inland with an oar over his shoulder until somebody asked, 'What's that?', Mary and I turned our backs on the sea, forgot about salt spray on the windows and sand in the bath, and moved inland to where trees could grow upright.

Yes, of course we miss the seaside and we enjoy revisiting it, but although we are not serious collectors of artefacts we have collected a host of happy memories. This late summer holiday in North Norfolk has revived many a memory for me, and some for both of us.

On the journey up here we paused in Thetford Forest – just one of the scenes from my early childhood. The Forestry Commission picnic sites are as oases in the desert; places of cool refreshment, lush green grass, mature trees, space and tranquillity. They are indeed about as different from motorway service stations as one can imagine. A flask of coffee and a sandwich in such settings become nectar and ambrosia.

On then to Castle Acre, where my fondest memories have always been of unbridged fords rather than the ruins of castle and priory, impressive though they are. In those far-off days I was taken in a car belonging to the parents of my friend Geoffrey, who was at Gresham's School in Holt. I believe that it was a Wolseley. It had wooden spokes to the wheels, wide running boards which could act as Plimsoll lines in those fords, and removable celluloid side windows. I think there was a two-gallon petrol can on one of the running boards.

Mary and I visited the one remaining ford down the lane towards South Acre, where the crystal clear waters of the Nar flow between ancient meadows. 'Unsuitable for Motors' read the sign; certainly suitable for refreshing happy memories.

Back up the hill to the remains of the priory – Cluniac, they tell me, the finest monastic remains in East Anglia. Much to our surprise we were entertained by Morris dancers, an energetic, happy troupe (if that is the correct collective noun) performing in such an amazing setting, bathed in the warm afternoon sunshine.

The sunshine didn't last. We had the firm impression that summer ended at 4 p.m. that day. Premature darkness, horizontal rain and wind such as we had been accustomed to at Pakefield greeted our arrival on the coast. Yet the next day we walked along the coastal path and lay on a grassy bank as warm as one could wish. When we opened our eyes we found that we were observed by a semi-circle of cows silently chewing their cuds. One felt compelled to stand and make a speech, but they were an unresponsive audience.

Time and the local authority have been kind to Blakeney. The only intrusive change has been the gross increase in traffic through its charming little streets, and the inevitable rash of yellow lines and notices. When I worked in Holt I sometimes came down here with my lunch-time sandwiches. I have known the quay and the creek in every kind if weather. Often in winter the whole scene turns grey; marsh, water, mud and sky merge. When the air is clear and a high sea has been running outside one may catch a glimpse of white breakers beyond the Pit and the marram grasses.

The Pit! What a pitiful name for such an expanse of water. Tide is the stage manager here, remorselessly flooding in to create a pool of heaven for the masses of small boats or slopping out again to reveal sand banks and acres of glorious, glistening mud. Woe betides the dinghy sailor who fails to make it back up the creek before the sluicing waters defeat him.

Blakeney is the last of the three ports left on the Glaven estuary, and is now open only for small boats. Some of the buildings around the quay area give an indication of former trading days. Embedded on the high tide line on the hard are the remains of a huge anchor. It is big enough to sink any boat that can now navigate the channel. The flood level marks for 1959 and 1978 are silent reminders that life is not always tranquil in this haven of peace.

The first time I was taken out to the Point I was introduced to fishing. We caught nothing but eels, and I was put right off the whole idea. I've never done any fishing since, except with a few hand grenades in the warm waters off the coast of North Africa.

It is hardly possible to spend time in Blakeney and some of the other coastal villages without becoming interested and inquisitive about cobblestones and flintwork. St Nicholas Church is about the only building to boast dressed flint, and not the best of examples to be found in the area. The other buildings and many boundary walls offer every possible pattern and every size of cobbles. I talked to a builder in Westgate Street, asking him if he worked in cobbles. 'Yes,' he said, 'and I love it.'

'Are there special names for the various sizes of stones?' I asked, and was disappointed that there seem not to be, that they are customarily referred to in inches, four inches being regarded as the standard. 'How boring,' I said, 'I felt sure there would be some good Norfolk words such as cobs, knobs, knockers, or even Nelsons.' He agreed, and decided that perhaps he would make some up ready for the next time somebody asked him.

Of course we had to go out to the Point to see the seals. Not to do so would be like going to Killarney and not kissing the Blarney Stone. I always

68

get the impression that the seals enjoy the entertainment as much as we do. They come and have a good look at the visitors before going back on the sand, where they roll about laughing!

On Sunday we went to the Antiques Fair in the Village Hall (one is never quite off-duty.) It was a somewhat lacklustre affair, with too much china, glass and lace for my taste. Only two stalls were of interest to me. One had a good mix of nonsense such as soldering irons, a Plunket roller and some medals, of which 'Pip, Squeak and Wilfred' were in good condition but with faded and stained ribbons. I noted that World War 1 medals were beginning to creep up in price. We didn't buy anything. By the time items have reached a Fair they have usually also reached their top price, but one looks and looks and lives in hope. The other interesting stall belonged to a friend from near home. Some of her better offerings could well have been bought from William.

Clearly I tempted the gods by mentioning those grey days. We left Blakeney at the end of our holiday in a storm of wind, torrential rain and with a high tide over the quay and across the street. If North Norfolk really is half way to Heaven, then Blakeney is one step on the road.

LOT 19
Neat but not gaudy

If indeed 'the apparel oft proclaims the man', I suppose that I am seen as one of varied interests, most of them of a practical nature. This is quite the reverse of my paternal grandfather, the solicitor, whom I always see in my mind's eye as the epitome of a city gentleman. I do not recall ever seeing him dressed other than in a dark suit, with highly polished shoes, a discreet amount of white lawn handkerchief showing at his breast-pocket and more often than not with a carnation in his lapel.

As children we were very much overawed by his appearance and military manner. His moustache and speech were clipped and precise. He was clearly ready to draw up a will at short notice or to convey a property (marked pink on the attached plan). The strange thing was that his fastidiousness and precision were oddly in contrast to the dusty gloom of his offices. It was that gloom which caused me at an early age to reject the possibility of joining the family firm. We can all look back on missed opportunities, and that was an early one on my part.

The apparel of my other grandfather was an entirely different matter. If the tweed of his suits and in particular of his Norfolk jacket proclaimed a country gentleman, they did no more than speak the truth. He was one of the most gentle men I have ever known. Like his father before him, he was the village doctor at New Buckenham.

For me he has always personified the very best in the old traditions of a country practitioner. He always wore a gold watch which he would produce from an inner pocket. It was as much a tool of his trade as his stethoscope in another pocket. He seemed always to be surrounded by an aura of quiet competence which inspired confidence in his patients as well as in his small grandson.

I have never been what you might call a snappy dresser except, perforce, when in uniform, and looking back I suppose one could call dinner jackets or tails uniform. It's a long time now since I wore either, and I don't propose to alter that situation. No one who had to wear one at school, as I did, could be expected to shed a tear at the demise of stiff starched collars. The only sad aspect of the matter is the thought of the swathe of industry that died with them.

In 1937 I was a management trainee at the Colchester Steam Laundry and Carpet Beating Company. At an early stage in my training I was given a hamper full of soiled stiff white collars and told to launder and dress them. As I recall, the task took me the best part of a week, after which I was told to go back to the beginning and do it all again.

The first problem in the process is to remove the old starch. Normal washing does not always succeed in doing this, and there are several courses open, including soaking them overnight before the washing process. By the Thirties the old mangle had been superseded by the centrifugal extractor, which eventually came to be known as the spin dryer. After 'extraction' the collars were placed in a machine called the Sunflower, rather like a wooden butter churn, containing the starch solution. There were many variations in the recipe for making up that solution, the basis of which was rice starch and borax. The specific gravity of the starch was measured with a specially calibrated hydrometer, invented by a Mr Twaddell – from whom we get our expression 'absolute twaddle'. I was, at a later date, the proud owner of a splendid brass Twaddell hydrometer, and now much regret its loss.

A second run in the extractor reduced the moisture content and the collars were then ready for blocking and polishing. The finishing machines that I knew consisted mainly of a gas heated roller revolving over a reciprocating padded board on which the collars were laid. The one that I can visualise most clearly had a name. It was called The Prince; the name and *fleur de lys* were picked out in gold paint on the cast iron frame which was also lined in the manner of coach-work, clearly demonstrating Victorian pride in craftsmanship. A 'liner' was indeed a specialist.

To the inexperienced the collar polishing machine was a brute to manage. I suppose that the hardest lesson I had to learn was not to become overwhelmed with embarrassment at forty or fifty females witnessing my ineptitude. (Later in my career at the laundry my mother said to me, 'David, are you doing a man's job?' to which I replied, 'Mother, I keep fifty women happy'.)

When blocked and polished, the collars had to be curled and shaped. There were various mechanical aids for this, but nothing was better than doing it by hand. The finished articles were placed in wicker trays and put into 'the stove', a small well heated and well ventilated room which got its name from the fact that it had originally housed a purpose-built cast iron stove on which the old flat-irons were heated.

The carpet-beating machine hinted at in the company name was truly archaic. I would not like to guess its date of origin and am inclined to think it was unique. It was driven by a gas engine, using gas from the town mains. A carpet was fed into it on moving canvas bands. Somewhere in its murky depths it was thumped and thrashed, and the resulting dross was expelled by extractor fans into the meadow at the rear of the building.

One other memory and social history note from those days concerns the laundry vans. Only the smartest and quietest van was allowed for collection and delivery in Frinton. Clacton was not quite so starchy.

Finding that objects familiar from one's childhood are now regarded as collectible bygones has a salutary effect. William was well pleased with two collar boxes and a stud box which he brought back from Newark last week. They were, I am certain, absolute duplicates of the ones I owned, beautifully made of leather with golden lettering in case one had any doubt about their purpose.

Closely allied to stiff collars were the ruffs worn by choirboys. I never attempted to master the art of goffering ruffs. The goffering irons made for the purpose were very similar to curling tongs, which preceded more complicated procedures for achieving 'permanent waves'. As I recall, the goffering irons were heated by being inserted in the circular hole in the rear of the gas-heated smoothing irons, or over the gas ring normally used for boiling a kettle. Like the tools of all dying crafts, these items have become harder to find, and have a firm place among today's bygones. Even the humble flat-iron finds it place on stalls at fairs. The No.7 is the most common; numbers above or below that datum line fetch higher prices.

From time to time we get a little homework handed out. Mary and I have a good track record for the restoration of those little chests of drawers, so they are given to us to deal with. I still undertake a very occasional rush-bottoming or more frequently sea-grassing a stool or chair. We used to sneer at sea-grass as a poor substitute for rush, but now accept that there are cases where it looks right, even if we don't actually like it.

Such jobs as these and small carpentry matters have highlighted the need for a workshop at home. I have been lucky to be able to take over a small utility room, complete with radiator. I have, as you might say, at last come in from the cold. This makes for greater comfort but creates a new problem. Sawdust escapes to the rest of the house – it gets everywhere and is not popular.

When we lived on the cliff at Pakefield we had a similar problem with sand. When friends came to stay, and if you live by the sea friends do come to stay, they were apt to say that they knew they were at the seaside because of the sand in the bottom of the bath. We tried to tolerate sand rather than fight it. It arrived in the house all through the summer in sandals, swimsuits, towels and any beach paraphernalia. With five in the family this could amount to quite a pile, and it is surprising how uncomfortable sand can be in the wrong places (ask anyone who served with the Eighth Army). Having moved away from the sandy seaside, we must now find an answer to intrusive sawdust.

Before I leave this domestic theme I must mention that Mary has a great dislike of having the sweep in the house. Her aversion dates right back to our early days in Pakefield and our first chimney sweep. He arrived with a pony and trap and in an advanced state of inebriation, swept with more enthusiasm than finesse and left a sorry mess behind him. What was the charge, I wonder? Probably about half-a-crown. It was before the days of Sweep-and-Vac, and I can't even be sure that we owned a suction cleaner of our own at the time. In any case, cleaning up soot by whatever means certainly raises a dust which settles on even the best shrouded furniture.

Chimney sweeping never caught on as a DIY activity, which wouldn't surprise you if you ever tried one method I have heard recommended, which was to fire both barrels of a shotgun up the chimney, and then sweep up. Alternatively, what they used to tell you to do in the country was to get a lump of holly-bush – not too big or it may get stuck, and then you are in real trouble. Porcupine holly is best, with its extra curly and pointed leaves. Tie it on a weighted line, get on the roof, drop the weight down the chimney, go indoors and haul the holly down, then sweep up!

The last sweep we had was a jolly red-haired giant; Bernard was his name. He gave me an interesting insight into his vocation.

'It was my Great Uncle Billy what show me how to sweep chimneys. "Come you on," he say to me, "I'm going to sweep your aunt's chimbley." Well, I weren't above nine or ten at the time. I was wide awake and I took it all in. You never saw such dirt and dust; that went everywhere. I say to myself, if I can't do better than that I aren't worth nothing. That's when I decided to be a sweep. Yes thank you, I would like a cup of tea or coffee, whatever you're having. Milk and sugar, please.'

That little monologue came back to me seeing a bundle of cane rods and a sweep's brush among the load of bygones we were getting ready for the sale room, and turned my thoughts to the roofs and chimneys which I see from my study window. Our nearest neighbours have thatches; one a good example of Norfolk reed, the other an altogether softer effect in straw. Looking up the gentle rise towards the huge copper beech which crowns the hill there is almost every sort of roof. Over the lane there is an example of machine-made pantiles, efficient, cost-effective and boring; its visual merit is that it plays the straight man to the comic irregularities of ancient pantiles on the old saddlery.

There are slate roofs of various pitch, which glisten after rain and change colour with the sky. Far from native products, but they have been here long enough to be accepted. All the various tiles are man-made, we are too far distant from natural stone to enjoy graduated tiles, but many, like those on the Chapel of Ease, are pleasantly flecked with lichen, and all are well mellowed.

Chimneys stand like sentinels in a tented encampment. Not all are graced with pots. Even these utilitarian objects are far from uniform; hardly any two are identical. They display individual artistry and design ranging from tall and slender to short and squat, fluted and fancy to severely plain. I would like to be able to relate them to their owners but that might be pushing fancy too far.

I wonder who first thought of chimney pots. My guess is that they first appeared in early Victorian times. Before that a chimney-stack had sufficed, and up to those times there were many remarkable and elaborate examples built. By reason of their nature, complete chimney stacks do not appear on the sale grounds where architectural sales are held, while almost every such sale will have some pots on offer, many of them remarkably beautiful objects when one is able to appreciate the finer points, hardly visible when up on high. It is no surprise to me that such pots have become desirable objects and garden features.

What I cannot explain is why, with such a choice available, the swifts have chosen our cottage for their summer residence. Each year we have been here they have returned to lay their eggs and raise their young on all four sides of our pantiled roof. After we moved in, we found that the cast-iron guttering needed to be replaced. We waited until the swifts had returned to Africa before having it replaced with black plastic, and hoped that this would not upset them when they returned the following year. Happily they accepted the change, and continued to thump into it as they disappeared under the tiles.

Swifts fly at such tremendous speed that we are unable to distinguish between young and old, but usually feel fairly sure that the nestlings have been launched when we note increased aerial activity. There is sometimes another clue. Our swifts give us so much pleasure that it seems churlish to mention the single unpleasant aspect of their tenancy of our roof. While in the nest the young play host to a parasite, a small bug with oversized feet, which they shed when leaving the nest. Occasionally one or two of these small creatures crawl down to our bedroom.

Mary's personal involvement with the swifts takes the form of a 'relaunch service'. On various occasions we have found one grounded in the yard and quite unable to take off. Mary dries their feathers with a tissue and keeps them in our airing cupboard until they are rested and looking ready. Then she launches them into the air from an upstairs window and has never failed to see them swoop up and rejoin the others. The only thanks Mary receives is some pricked fingers from their needle-sharp claws.

As birds are on the agenda this is the moment to tell a little story about 'the sparrow who lived at No.7'. The incidents occurred when we lived at the Old Forge, where there was a pantiled extension to the rear of the thatched cottage. A pair of sparrows had made their nest beneath the seventh tile from the corner. Unfortunately the mother sparrow couldn't count. Every time she landed on the gutter she hopped along sideways, looking beneath the tiles for number seven, and often caused offence to other inhabitants. Mary couldn't stand this foolish behaviour for long. She clipped a clothes peg to the gutter outside No.7, and you will have to believe me when I say that thereafter the mother always went straight home. And by the way, did I ever mention that Mary is a former kindergarten mistress?

Alphabet of Advice for Antiques-sellers

Apparel – *provenance of clothing affects value. Uniforms and stage costumes are good bets.*

Bracket feet may be missing from furniture; replacement restores a look of importance.

China – *the smallest of defects affects value.*

Dolls – *beyond my ken.*

Elbowgrease – *there is no real substitute.*

Fish – *stuffed fish can fetch silly prices.*

Gold – *just dream about it.*

Hand tools from ancient trades are well worth seeking.

LOT 20
Royal Norfolk Show

I am always happy to watch a craftsman at work, but I don't often get the chance to lie in bed and watch a thatcher. He made an early start, which is something I don't often do these days, so there he was within a few feet, up his ladder, removing the old netting from the ridge of Cherry Tree House, the other side of the lane from my bedroom window.

In a very short time the place was a shambles. Dirty straw and the remnants of netting and broaches drifted down into the lane. When I got downstairs I could see that he had only brought straw for the job - no reeds, which confirmed my suspicion that this was not to be a full re-thatching but only a re-capping. This was a pity, as there are few occupations I enjoy more than watching a reed thatch grow like magic beneath a thatcher's hands. I like the way in which the yelms lose their individuality as they are patted into place and become a part of the whole thatch, almost, as one might say, like raw recruits being accepted and drilled to become essential components of an efficient unit. Straw never looks as if discipline will be achieved. Right up to the very last minute it has a Thelwellian, dishevelled look to it, and then suddenly there is well-groomed neatness and order. I've seen it all before, but only when, for a brief spell, I became a thatcher's assistant have I had such a close-up view of the whole job which was going on forty feet from my bedroom window.

When I commented recently how out of place aluminium ladders and steel scaffolding look on a thatching job, I realised that I was not the one to make such comments, with fourteen power tools in the workshop, and considering the fact that I had just re-hung the doors of a mid-Victorian corner cupboard using a cordless electric screwdriver.

We were puzzled that first week by the thatcher's erratic appearances and then two days' absence. Mary and I went to the Royal Norfolk Show and all was explained; there he was, giving demonstrations of Norfolk reed thatching.

One of the reasons we like to go the Show is that William takes a couple of days off from normal routine and assumes the role of Steward. He also assumes a smart suit and a bowler hat, the latter requiring a good haircut; the full ensemble is quite impressive. The parts of the Show I like best are the livestock and the rural industries. It looks almost impossible for a judge to find fault with any one of the (to my eye) perfect specimens presented and paraded for inspection. But somehow it is done, and rosettes are awarded. The cattle return stoically to their beds of straw; the sheep are more animated and the pigs rumbustious. In these PC days, I hardly like to mention that my favourite cattle are British Whites.

One of the fascinations of the rural industries part of the show is that there are people actually doing things, always so much better than a static display of machinery, however awe-inspiring. Better too than an array of cars, which one can see any day in a showroom and probably test drive. And who, I wonder, goes to the show to buy a Jacuzzi bath, a watercolour painting, a potted plant or a summer dress?

Perhaps somebody does. Anyhow, I was delighted to have a chat with the thatcher before moving on to watch a demonstration of sheep-shearing – not unlike those last moments of thatching when an unruly shaggy mass suddenly becomes a well-trimmed product. But oh the indignity of being clamped in a half-Nelson and having the clippers run all over one's body! I don't actually enjoy even a 'short back and sides'.

On then to the blacksmith, the ring of hammer on anvil as clear and distinctive as church bells, and the pure magic of beating hot metal into an infinite range of shapes: a hook, a latch, a ram's head, pokers and door fittings. Some of his products were purely ornamental – or at least I was not able to stretch my mind to find a use to which they could have been put. What I think of as the real work of a smith has largely disappeared. Long gone are the days when he would have been kept busy all day at harvest time making new parts to keep the work of the harvest moving. At other times there were tools to be made, repaired or sharpened and sometimes ornamental work – gates, weathervanes, perhaps a sundial or a beautiful well-head.

Today's farrier is more likely to arrive in a Land Rover, with a mobile, gas-operated forge, and to carry out his business on site rather than in a forge. But the essential sights and smells of the scene remain unchanged after countless generations. Have any of today's farriers shod oxen, I wonder? So far as I know the last oxen used in the fields made their exit before the last World War, in Wiltshire.

When we bought the Old Forge we were disappointed to find so few things left by its former occupant. There was plenty of evidence of its former use: the blackened chimney, a nail-encrusted bench and those wonderful blackened bellows, but no water trough, not a single tool, and most noticeably no anvil. We later found the anvil in the mill on the other side of the road, but though we searched diligently, even using a metal detector, we found no other artefacts, not even the tyre ring.

In the course of time we were told many stories about the last smith who had worked there. Then one afternoon, he and his wife walked in. They joined us for a cup of tea, and his wife filled us in on many of the details we had longed to know. He was not a talker, a quiet, gentle man, thoroughly steeped in our East Anglian habit of reticence and understatement. How long was it since he last shod a horse? 'Ah! Quite some time.'

At the Show, we lingered quite a long time with the blacksmith before moving on to watch a bodger expertly turning spindles on a primitive lathe. A woodland craft this, not much associated with East Anglia, more to be found in the beech woods of Buckinghamshire, turning out components by the thousand for Windsor chairs. I wish I had asked if this type of lathe can be adapted for turning hollow-ware.

The hurdle-maker was our next entertainment – one of those jobs which is made to look deceptively easy in the hands of an expert. We found a fine display of his work, but the man himself was missing, so we moved on to watch the activities of wattle fence-making. Our last pleasure in that section of the show was the chair-maker's stand. His chairs were truly beautiful. So often I feel that hand-crafted objects, be they chairs, gates, stools or whatever, are over-ornamented, the maker being unable to resist another curlicue, excessive turnery or some other extravagance which spoils the design. Here the chairs on display, and those on which he was doing a little gentle polishing, had nothing to detract from their simplicity of line. Some looked as if they were influenced by Shaker ancestors, while others clearly derived from the Windsor chair-makers of High Wycombe. Beech wood predominated, all being finished in their natural colour, beautiful to touch and a pleasure to behold. Some of his chairs were rush seated to the highest possible standard, a standard which I freely admit I have never reached, but which earns my full admiration. Rushwork was one of those skills which I acquired along the way. It is an occupation which has given me enormous pleasure, as I have applied it to a range of delightful chairs, mostly ladder-backs, some of them rockers – one a remarkable triangular-seated job which I remember as being very taxing – and a variety of stools, the most pleasurable being oblong ones and the most difficult being round ones.

An enchanting aspect of rushwork has been when William and I have been able to take time off to go and harvest rushes in pretty places such as Shelly or Wissington. I must not get carried away, as I am sure I have detailed such expeditions elsewhere.

Our day at the show had been a tiring one. In our experience it usually is, as well as being very hot or very wet – rarely a day of moderation. Oddly enough, I have the same feeling about the sale ground at Aylsham, where it has often been too hot or too cold for comfort, with too many hours spent watching the parade of humanity and too few moments of worth, with small triumphs spread over a catalogue of perhaps nine hundred lots. One hot day, Mary and I found cool refreshment down by the mill at the other end of Aylsham. The contrast offered by a glade so green and cool after the dusty heat of the sale room was almost as sharp as if we had actually plunged into the water. Three small fishermen, the youngest I have ever watched but with gear more sophisticated than I have ever handled, made a few half-hearted casts and were more interested in a large container of orange squash and a bag of food. Two young men arrived on commendably quiet motorbikes, stripped off and plunged into the pool. An artist, still as a heron in a reed-bed, sat sketching the ivy-covered warehouse. A woman emerged from her cottage to feed some geese. A party of four came gliding along from Anchor Bridge. They pulled their boat out on to the grass and walked away, declaring that they had earned themselves some long cool drinks.

After an hour or so there was no more human activity, but the scene continued to be one of animation. The tail race frothed and chuckled. The last rays of the sun were reflected as dappled patches of light on willow and alder. A young harnser jerked his way home to roost and moor hens were active around the fringes of the pool, busy as cleaners in a deserted conference room. As the light faded there was welcome relief, and a feel of overdue rain was in the air.

It seems strange that a town that traded and prospered by means of the river for well over a hundred years now appears almost entirely dissociated from it. But Aylsham is by no means unique in this. As we travel around in and beyond East Anglia we often notice how it has frequently been the custom for most towns to turn their backs on their rivers, treating them as drains or rubbish tips rather than as life-giving arteries. But I must be fair. The tranquil spot which gave us so much pleasure that evening is made so largely by the trees. They frame glimpses of the old mill, and entirely obliterate the modern buildings. They overhang the water, willow tendrils trailing romantically, forming havens for wildlife and a haunt for squirrels, but what wherryman in need of a breeze would have tolerated them? In what might have been called its heyday this might have been an almost treeless waste, vandalised in the name of progress, scorned by artists and writers of prose. Only now has it become a haven for peaceful pleasure and serene contemplation. None of this proves anything; it is only what one might call 'reflections on the Bure'.

I note that since that day the mill has been put to a new use. Like many barns and farm buildings it has been adapted for domestic use, in this case a number of self-contained holiday apartments.

I have another, less blissful, memory of Aylsham sale ground. Out on the grass I had successfully bid for two massive blacksmith's bellows. Strange to relate, when I came to load them up the crowd of potential helpers had melted away, and I had to struggle with them on my own.

It's a long time since we had a set of blacksmith's bellows to work on. They are so rewarding of the effort. Almost without exception they consist of two huge slabs of elm, darkened by age and use to Stygian hues, and the leather which connects them black as the metal spout. Their massive strength proclaims their fitness of purpose, symbolic of the best qualities which we attribute to the village blacksmith. With diligence we are able to clean the leather work, using saddle-soap to restore suppleness. The slabs of elm return to a rich honey colour, soaking up wax polish and eventually being returned to a glossy finish.

Who bought these beautiful objects from us? Usually Americans, possibly with ranch houses in Texas with plenty of room, as we gleaned that they were most likely to be used as coffee tables. I am never foolish enough to ask why people buy things. With these lovely objects, as with so many of the bygones that we sell, their beauty alone is sufficient to engender possessiveness.

'If in doubt, do nowt'; over-cleaning is always a mistake.

Junk – One man's junk is another man's treasure.

Knobs – as with handles these should be in period.

Loose joints are a real turn-off. Fix them.

Musical instruments are best left to the experts.

Nelson and nautical memorabilia are always a good bet.

Over-mantels and other architectural items are of great interest.

Pearls improve when worn next to the skin.

Quote realistic prices when selling. Everyone now expects a discount.

LOT 21
Trash and Treasure

We learned from the *East Anglian Daily Times* that the Hoxne Treasure would be on display in Ipswich for only one more week. Mary's diary was full so I decided to go alone. I set out early, intending to drive to Ipswich to see the Treasure at the museum. Just beyond Brockford, a cock pheasant walked out into the road. There was a car coming in the opposite direction so I couldn't swerve. Half way over the road he changed direction and tried to get back. I hit him fair and square. He shattered the plastic number plate, went straight into the air duct and punched a hole in the radiator. Suddenly I was driving a steam engine with feathers and boiling water splattering around under the bonnet.

I was lucky to be near a Ford garage and still luckier that they had a replacement radiator in stock. 'Two hours', they said. I accepted the estimate in the optimistic manner in which it was offered, changed into my boots and set off with the dog for a walk.

This was new ground to me and I had no map. In the strange, misty morning light all was not as it seemed at first. The silhouette of a church with a low stumpy spire turned out to be a grain store – another Alston enterprise, I noted. The clan must have come south and quietly taken over half of Suffolk one day when we were looking the other way.

The village, when I reached it, was fine delight. Even the large burial ground had an air of happiness rather than sadness, with collar doves calling from the headstones. The church was a sad, damp beauty with a smell of decay. It was locked, 'key at Post Office'. As it was not yet nine o'clock I walked the village street and was enchanted by the small thatched cottage in the corner of the churchyard. Hard to believe that it could have been a mill in such a situation, but the evidence of the spillway emerging from under the building was irrefutable. School and schoolhouse rested in the unnatural peace of half term; clearly its pupils are bussed in from local villages to fill its classrooms and enjoy its playing field.

Back then to the Post Office, which I knew I had to visit, for I have never seen one more attractive, and going in I was in no way disappointed. The pretty cottage, with blue shutters now removed from the bay window, was a delight. A proper bell tinkled as I opened the door and stepped in; low beams were inches above my head; there were brass scales, a mahogany counter, pigeonholes on the wall, a clerk's desk with turned balusters, a Windsor scroll-backed armchair for the convenience of customers; all were perfectly in accord with the warm welcome I received.

Here was a Post Office that my mother or even my grandmother would have recognised and appreciated. I am sure that had I asked for one second class stamp it would have been dispensed with a smile. Perhaps the fact that I came away knowing the charming post-mistress by her Christian name shows how easily the conversation flowed – I also know her age, and you will not expect me to reveal that either.

Who could fail to be enchanted by the story of the three ladies who used to live in the former mill which I had admired? Two occupied the ground floor, the third lived upstairs. Well no, not strictly upstairs but up a ladder, and it was considered most improper that she was in constant danger of displaying her underwear while climbing up and down. Or if that failed to tickle the imagination there was the short history of the bogus clergyman who occupied the vicarage for a time. It had required an Act of Parliament to legalise three marriages which he had performed before being exposed.

I would much have liked to sit in the Windsor chair and hear more, but felt obliged to say my farewells. The old dog and I resumed our walk. We followed a footpath between the old church and some houses set among trees tinged with autumn colours. A stout wooden footbridge over a ditch brought us to the edge of plough land, freshly turned and gleaming like chocolate. Autumn may well be the season of mellow fruitfulness, it is also the season of fruity smells. From my youthful days on the farm I can usually identify the products of piggeries and stockyard; I am less sure about inorganics.

Eventually, with the sun warm on our backs, we headed back by narrow roads and sunken lanes. The old dog scented something in the ditch. The poor old thing had missed out on fertilisers, rabbits, squirrels, pheasants, partridge and pigeon, but homed in unfailingly on a jettisoned fish and chip paper. I must not underrate her too grossly, for she actually led me to an interesting find in the ditch; a Doulton water-filter (pre-1901), broken it is true, but not beyond repair. I never got to the museum that day, but truly one man's trash is another man's treasure.

Mary and I found a real trash and treasure shop over in that direction on another expedition. We were staying for a few days at Woodbridge, a little town which always gives me pleasure. Combining the merits of a country town with a seaport, it proves to be a happy hunting ground for agricultural and nautical antiques. I had been reading *East Coast Rivers* by Lt. Mussen, R.N. He vividly describes and gives practical advice on entering the mouth of the river Deben and fetching up to a safe anchorage at Woodbridge Quay. He then adds that it is possible to proceed further, but that '...it could serve no practical purpose.' This is a sailor's point of view, conditioned by salt water and the need to have a fathom or two under one's keel. From the point of view of an East Anglian wishing to visit a delicious slice of Suffolk, a brief journey up the valley could hardly be bettered.

It is, admittedly, not a journey to be undertaken in a boat. As the gallant lieutenant indicated, navigation by all but the smallest craft ceases at Wilford Bridge. Nor did the East Suffolk railway give thought to such possibilities when they cut Woodbridge off from its waterfront and pressed on up the shallow valley towards Campsea Ash, passing low over the water three times in as many miles.

The whole 15-mile meander up to Debenham can be completed on roads so quiet that they offer pleasant walking. At Lower Street, Ufford, one of its two churches is now declared redundant, but the Church of the Assumption in the centre of the village tells a very different story. The building and its contents are a commentary on our history since the times of the Normans, with some comments typically East Anglian, such as the mixed stone and flint work and the 15th century carved oak benches. Our remarks about the 18th century stocks and whipping post were not entirely in accord with today's less robust attitudes.

Down the street, beyond the Lion, we crossed the twin bridges over the Deben and lingered to watch the inevitable small boy fishing. We speculated on the age of the immense willows by the water. A swan glided by in solitary regal fashion, hardly giving us a glance. It was clearly a superior breed to the shameless beggars we had been feeding earlier, down by the tide mill.

The river is a little secretive between here and the old mill at the site of Ash Abbey. There was one heart-sinking moment on the approach from Ufford when it seemed inevitable that the rural lane would be eclipsed by the Wickham Market bypass, but all was well, and the holiday traffic streamed by a few yards away as we veered off and continued our leisurely way. Ash Abbey is one of those delightful places of which one gets fleeting glimpses from the train. I had seen it thus many times before I managed to reach it on foot. On this return visit it was no less beautiful and we paused happily to watch a competent mother duck supervising a flotilla of thirteen downy chicks.

Below Wickham Market the stream still flows strongly. We grow accustomed to learning that 'a mill is recorded on this site in the Domesday Book' and we never doubt it. They are the most purposeful of buildings and always seem to be set in exactly the right place. We were charmed by the wickerwork displayed by the bridge, and equally by the oven-fresh bread available on the other side of the road. Going on up the valley, we were rarely more than a few miles from the infant Deben, now hardly reckoned to be a river except in winter. Here, as often along our route, the trees met above our heads to form a leafy tunnel.

Debenham would probably not claim to be the most beautiful village in Suffolk; the competition is too strong. But it does have a dishevelled charm, and it has not one but three antique shops, so whatever Lieutenant Musson thought about it, our journey served a very practical purpose, besides being a day of enchantment and rural bliss. The first shop we visited was a treasure house indeed, devoted to architectural features. Not really our line of country, but fascinating nevertheless. The second, an antiques centre actually, was devoted almost exclusively to furniture. That suits me well; I do not have the knowledge or interest in glass or china which dominates so many centres. But show me furniture, especially country style, pine, wickerwork, rushwork, craft tools, and I am happy. Our most profitable finds were in the third shop. I cannot now recall the whole list of our purchases, but it certainly included cow-keeps, rat-traps of various sorts, stools, a heavy oak chest and a corn bin with the regulation rat-holes in the bottom corners. When one strikes a rich vein, one keeps going back for another pick. We had to go back the next day with the car to collect our booty.

We did not seek out the source of the little trickle beside the street that grows to be the river Deben. As often happens, local opinion is divided on the exact location, but if you say firmly, 'up Aspall way', then you cannot be wrong. Mary and I returned to base and watched the harvest moon ride clear of Sutton Hoo. It lit the valley where the masts in the marina stood in the mist like a stricken forest.

When we went back the next day there were two more surprises waiting for us. First there were two ladies producing impeccable rushwork seats and other items from Debenham Rushweavers. The second was almost too good to be true. We found an old friend of mine from North Norfolk. I used to see Frank working on the osier bed down the lane from our house. He was the last in his family to make a living as a basket-maker. Each year he came to cut osiers, and bit by bit I had learned about his trade and its history. So far as he could say, the family had been basket-makers from way back. 'Wouldn't even be surprised if one of them hadn't made that there basket for little old Moses, 'cept of course that were made of rushes. Not that I can't turn my hand to a bit of rushwork. Fact a spell on rush work gives your hands a rest, they're not so hard to handle as what osiers are. I worked for my uncle; he wasn't an easy man. I was properly apprenticed. Even though I worked something hard for a few shillings a week, I couldn't have had a better training. The hardest thing at first was the shop board you sat on down on the floor and the lap board which you worked on. It was always funny cold in the workshop. I don't believe we even had no heating. If that had been too warm the osiers would have dried out and got too brittle.'

Frank told me about the osier bed down the lane. He had helped his uncle to plant it and two or three more around the area. You needed plenty of moisture in the ground, he said, like this one; it was actually an advantage if it got flooded during the winter. The 'sets' for planting were nothing more than willow sticks, they were stuck in the ground about three or four feet apart in rows. They were cut every year, the stump getting bigger and producing more shoots each season. Early in the New Year was the time for cutting. Freshly cut, the bark couldn't be peeled off, so they tied them in bundles which they stood in a wet ditch for perhaps three or four months. The sap would begin to rise in them and then they could be taken to the shop as required for peeling, a job done by pulling them through a cleaver. Peeled osiers were used for the better class of basket, the 'browns' (unpeeled) were used for cheaper baskets for fish, fruit and vegetables. Frank said that while he was still working with his uncle nearly all the baskets were made to order. They didn't carry any stock to speak of. Later on, when he became his own master, basketry was beginning to be ousted from its dominating position in the packaging of goods, so he found it necessary to diversify and reorientate his business towards retail outlets and to producing what he called fancy goods.

I told Frank of my earlier interests in the laundry industry. 'Ah! yes,' he said, 'Laundry hampers wasn't one of the easiest. I can still tell you the most popular size, it was 27 x 18 x 12 inches. My old dog Pip like getting a chew at the rawhide we used to bind those hampers.'

'And what are you doing now you are retired?' I asked.

'I don't do much at all,' he said, but that could hardly have been true, as he showed us his market garden, which looked flourishing, and told us that he sold most of his produce from a stall at the weekly market in Woodbridge.

Soon after these events, Mary brought home a leaflet called *Hedgerow Baskets*. Packed full of useful information and instructions, it really makes me feel that I would like to have a go. The list of potential materials reads like a walk down a good country lane; it includes Dogwood, Winter Jasmine, Larch, Sloe, Honeysuckle, Wild Rose, Ivy, Clematis and Virginia Creeper. I also note that, as with any ancient craft, there is a good sprinkling of special terms and obscure words: side stakes, base stakes, weavers, waling, randing and pairing. The age of a hedgerow can be approximately gauged by the number of hedging varieties in a given length. Perhaps the antiquity of a craft can be judged by the number of special words it takes under its wing.

LOT 22
Locks and quays

William claims to own the shortest railway line in East Anglia. He is probably right. It is about three and a half inches long, being in fact a section cut from a rail. Somehow I don't think that it will be much in demand among the railway buffs, but you never can tell.

For me the romance went out of the railways with the passing of the age of steam. I have never been able to raise much enthusiasm for diesel or electrics, and the thought of travelling at 200 mph across France or under the English Channel fills me with dismay.

Over the years we have handled a fair range of railway memorabilia: a great variety of signs from 'Station Master' to 'GENTLEMEN', 'Bovril brightens up old buffers' to 'Passengers will please refrain...', lamps, whistles, flags and even a large elaborate set of pigeonholes for holding stick-on instruction labels: Livestock, P.L.A., Fragile, etc., and a variety of destinations which are now miles from their nearest railway station.

I used to be taken to Mundesley for holidays - a place full of delightful early memories such as catching shrimps and cooking them over a driftwood fire down on the beach. The Poppy Line served the North Norfolk towns and villages for a brief span of about eighty years and has left nothing but a few embankments, a few rusting girder bridges and cuttings which serve no more noble purpose than sites for controlled tipping. The happiest thought that they give me is that of future archaeologists engaged in interesting digs among the debris of the throwaway plastic age.

Mary and I went on a day trip to Southwold with the Young Wives' Club (I have noted elsewhere that they were indeed 'Young Wives' forty or fifty years ago). As we went down the valley of the Blyth from Halesworth I gazed over the pastoral scene and mulled over the fact that two commercial highways along the valley had come and gone in the space of two generations. The narrow gauge railway (36 and one-sixth inches) connected Halesworth and Southwold, with stations at Wenhaston, Blythburgh and Walberswick. It is possible to trace most of its former course, and the last section provides a delightful walk beside and crossing the River Blyth, with the white lighthouse at Southwold like a guiding beacon.

Indeed, the greatest pleasure I derive from railways these days is walking along abandoned routes. A great asset for elderly walkers is the gentleness of all the inclines. The relics of the M.&G.N. offer some splendid examples in North Norfolk and I remember with pleasure other such walks in the Stour valley, a little branch line recorded for posterity by the American author, John Appleby, in *Suffolk Summer*. One can almost smell the smoke and feel the 'clickety-click' on the rails in his description of his journey and arrival at Cockfield. The additional charm of his book, now in its tenth reprint, is that he requested that the royalties should go towards the upkeep of the Old English Rose Garden in the Abbey gardens at Bury St Edmunds, as a permanent memorial to the American servicemen who gave their lives in the cause of freedom.

The charming little museum at Southwold has a section devoted to the defunct railway, among it a piece of rail possibly a couple of inches longer than William's unidentified portion. Memorabilia from the Southwold Railway is in short supply, but from the former River Blyth Navigation it is even more elusive if not actually totally missing.

Dereliction of canals was a national malady in the latter half of the eighteen hundreds. A saving grace in East Anglia has been the way in which they have been assimilated back into the landscape. Almost all our short navigations were achieved by canalising existing rivers and streams. This dealt more kindly with the landscape than the major engineering works of Thomas Telford's 'cut and fill' operations, or even the contour-following canals more typical of Brindley. Where little waterways were canalised, like the Blyth, which has only four locks in its nine miles down from Halesworth, the valley has been able to revert to a tranquil beauty of Constable quality.

Likewise the upper reaches of the River Bure, which strangely was also a nine-mile navigation. From Aylsham it dropped through six locks and passed five water mills on its leisurely way down to Coltishall. Here too the natural course of the river was followed, with the exception of a few short cuts to avoid sharp bends, or for passing the mills.

The New Cut at Reedham is the only significant length of artificial waterway in Norfolk and Suffolk. It is a reminder of the ambitious scheme to link Lowestoft and Norwich. Mutford lock is the sole remaining working lock in the whole area. The remains of Geldeston lock now mark the upper limit of navigation on the Waveney, which formerly linked Bungay to the system and was used by the wherry *Albion*.

I get as much pleasure from seeking out such industrial antiques as from portable objects which I might be tempted to buy and collect. Seeking them out leads one to some interesting places and some curious stories, like the time when Mary and I went looking for the Horstead canals and marl pits. We were not surprised that we found no one in Horstead who could point the way, as the workings were closed well over a hundred years ago. We took a walk out towards the oddly named area of 'Little Switzerland'. Beyond Heggatt Hall we left the road and followed a sandy track, silver sand, clean from the recent rain and bright with acorns from mature oaks. Passing a stand of mixed woodland, alive with game, we pressed on and came to High-Low bridge. Here the track is gated. We had arrived at our objective.

At first sight this strange bridge appears to span a railway cutting, flooded and overgrown. In fact the high arch carries the farm track over the first of a number of channels which were cut into the chalk hillside to give wherries access to the working faces. It is strange to follow the chain of cause and effect and to discover that the Emperor Napoleon was ultimately responsible for this extensive industrial development in the depths of the Norfolk countryside.

The riverside quarries were developed at the beginning of the nineteenth century, and as the face of the chalk which sloped gently down to the river Bure was cut back, so the channels were dug further and further. Eventually they reached fully half a mile into the area behind Wroxham Hall. All this effort was given impetus by the needs of a country at war, by the farmers using increasing quantities of marl for top-dressing their land, by the growing consumption of lime-kilns and the demands of cement works. All these enterprises were served direct by wherries. The great windmill at Berney Arms was originally built to provide power for a cement works, and probably drew its supplies from Horstead as well as from the Thorpe pits further up the river Yare.

I ought to know more about lime-kilns, for the early years of my life were spent within a few hundred yards of one. It was not actually in sight; the gentle slope of the field on the opposite side of Newmarket Road hid it from view. We sometimes played in the field, mostly around the roots of two huge elm trees and only moving up on to the slope when there was snow for our sledges. I am sure that we were warned away from the pit on the sensible grounds of danger, so if you will believe that I was a paragon of virtue then of course I never went near it! Certainly the two dark-mouthed caves in the working face of the chalk were both forbidden and forbidding; their gaping mouths wonderful stimulus for imagination and improbable local legend. No story could better the true one about the discovery in the Horstead pits of the skeleton of a Mastodon. The regrettable part of that episode is that when the scientists arrived on the scene the skeleton had been removed with the chalk and burnt for lime.

Our more recent enjoyment of canals and quarries has been further from home. When I say that the local teleffon [sic] directory devoted thirty pages to 'Jones', you will guess that Mary and I had been spending a few days in Wales. Llangollen is one of my favourite towns. So many places turn their backs on a river, but not this one. The Dee is the beautiful artery running through and giving life to the place. The canal, so unexpectedly found up the hillside, is also unexpectedly beautiful with its tree-shaded towpath down towards Froncysylite or up to the Horseshoe Falls. It was probably an ugly scar when it was first constructed and used as a commercial highway. Now, like a good antique, it is mellow and gives great pleasure to a lot of people.

Even in such a place, with so much demanding our attention, we are unable to resist the lure of a good 'den of antiquity', and sure enough there was one, tucked in behind the mill just above the bridge. Of the countless similar places I have browsed round I cannot think of one to offer such variety. There was everything from a crescent-shaped high backed settle to an aluminium ladder (though I am not sure that the latter was actually for sale), including a turtle shell, military medals, a suit of armour, primitive chairs, prints featuring the Prince of Wales when young and much, much

89

more. What I was looking for and expecting to find was a shepherd's crook. But no! And when I enquired the proprietor seemed to be completely baffled, as if he couldn't imagine why anyone except a shepherd would want one. The incident reminded me of the occasion when one of Mary's cousins who was also in the antiques business in Sheffield came to visit us at the Old Forge. He noticed a wooden wash-dolly, for which we had a steady demand, and said, 'I wouldn't dare show one of those in my shop. They still use them around us.'

Among a galaxy of metal objects I spotted a pair of miners' lamps, Davy safety lamps. Nothing in the shop had price tickets, so without much hope I asked the price. To my surprise the proprietor asked such a reasonable sum that I quite forgot to haggle. I was even more pleased when it emerged that he was asking the sum for the pair, not each. Perhaps he was an ex-miner and couldn't bear the sight of them.

Sir Humphrey Davy invented the safety lamp about 1800. I judged this pair to be at least a hundred years later. Like so many artefacts from the early nineteen hundreds, which can now certainly be described as antiques, those lamps reminded me of an early experience. During my annual stay at Holly Bush Farm, Uncle Jim always arranged one special treat for Geoffrey and me. One year it was a trip to the Wrekin, another was an unforgettable visit to a coal mine. I don't remember the name of the pit; it was a deep one, and the first amazing experience was going down in the cage. It dropped so fast that when it slowed the pressure on one's feet made it feel as though one was going up. Even more amazing was the reverse experience when returning to the surface.

We were supplied with helmets and safety lamps, and walked to various galleries including the working coal face and, most memorably, the pit ponies. They were clearly well loved and cared for. My overall impression of the pit was that of a warm friendly place, quite different from my expectations and quite different from another pit to which I was taken more recently. This second pit was a disused one kept open as a tourist attraction. It was cold and uninviting. Gone were those user-friendly wooden pit-props, replaced by steel girders, sheet metal and a multitude of powerful jacks. Gone long ago were pit ponies, replaced by endless belt conveyors. Gone was the restricted space at the coal face, replaced by huge mechanical cutters to pulverise the coal – not a decent lump in sight. But there you are, it's all very well for one to romanticise, quite another if one had to work down there for one's daily bread.

LOT 23
Mantraps and memories

The main thrust in the workshop this week was towards the periodic special sale of bygones. These events have become a regular feature in the year's programme , and seem to come round with remarkable speed.

William had a fairly large assembly set aside, and I thought an exceptionally good one. There were three baker's peels, each about eight feet long, two of them with flexible metal blades, the third one a wooden example. The last time I saw such a thing being used was while on holiday in Greece. The little bakery was so small that when the baker was wielding his peel the back end of it came out of the open window, a hazard for unwary pedestrians. The bakery was up an alley round behind one of the churches. It took me two days before I found it, and another to arrive at the right time to be served. His bread was worthy of even greater efforts.

About the same length as the peels was a thatcher's knife; all the shafts were straight-grained ash, smooth-worn with use and needing only a wipe over with a cloth. A light dusting of rust on the metal parts was easily removed.

There were other tools from other trades: a peat cutter, a selection of dibbers, three cromes, a brace of hay forks, a wooden hay rake undoubtedly a product of the old rake factory at Welneatham, baiting riddles and a cracking good flail, one of the most beautifully contrived and preserved that I have handled.

The *pièce de résistance* was a mantrap. This was truly horrific, fully five feet long, black, ugly and menacing – not a nice thing to meet in daylight, still less on a moonless night in the woods. In essence it is an enlarged version of a rat-trap with great jagged jaws which look as if they would snap a leg clean off rather than merely clamp onto it. An additional horror, in my eyes, was the large ring by which the trap would be securely tethered in case the victim should try to drag himself away.

Inevitably this gruesome exhibit, which I handled with care and some revulsion, despite the prospect of it running up to a sizeable winning bid at auction, reminded me of my first encounter with a poacher. This event occurred down on the marshes near Beccles. It was in reality a small theatrical performance staged for our credulous entertainment. Our host was Mr Garrood of Eliot and Garrood, Engineers, the man who invented the steam capstan which must have revolutionised the work on drifters and trawlers. My friend Geoffrey and I were hugely excited when we heard shots being fired and saw the chase and scuffle as two keepers overpowered and brought in the 'poacher'. The 'poacher' was then forced to lead us to his encampment, where we boiled a kettle for tea on his campfire and ate smoke-flavoured pieces of buttered toast.

Mr Garrood owned a steam-powered Broads cruiser named *Frolic*, of which I remember very little beyond its well-polished brass funnel. Many years later I made some abortive attempts to trace the *Frolic*. My enquiries produced one witness who claimed to have seen the vessel at an unspecified date with a motorbike on its deck, and who also said that it had been used by a film company making a film of *Huckleberry Finn*. Some vivid imagination must have been needed to portray the river Waveney as the Mississippi.

There was one other item to be worked on this morning which related to poaching or trespassing; a very simple little device, which, when activated by a tripwire, would fire a cartridge into the ground and thus give warning of unauthorised entry to the property. I feel confident that use of the mantrap has been illegal for many years, but can easily visualise marketing the tripwire device to a wide section of property owners.

I note that the mantrap and the gamekeeper's warning device both sold well; £550 for the one and £40 for the other. (I don't usually mention prices in these notes. Time moves on at such a speed, and together with inflation can make such statements seem ludicrously out of date.) There was some talk among the crowd that it might not actually have been a mantrap. Someone said that were signs on the 'platform' of the means of affixing bait. If this was true, it could have been a bear-trap, almost certainly imported into this country from northern Spain or eastern Europe. We will never know, and I doubt if the price would have been affected one way or the other.

Time in the workshop today was almost entirely devoted to a massive twelve-drawer chest of drawers. William had already stripped off all the paint, and beautiful warm weather had ensured that it was well dried. Cold wet weather is a great handicap; if not dried off quickly moisture tends to soak into the wood, prolonging the drying-out period. The laborious process of rubbing down took us through to elevenses time. Half of the top needed to be removed in order to close up a gap which had clearly developed over years of shrinkage. With this replaced, and the glue drying, we dealt with the drawer handles, replacing the especially uninspiring wood strip type with brass hoods – not cheap, but well worthwhile as they lifted the whole aspect of the piece from humdrum to that of a desirable object. The choice of handles and knobs is often a matter for discussion. We rarely, if ever, disagree, and it is truly remarkable what a difference the final selection can make to the general character and appearance of the piece of furniture. It's not unlike an identikit; swap around some eyebrows, give or take a moustache or a pair of jug ears and you have a different person whom you might or might not wish to have in your home.

After lunch it was waxing and polishing, which is also a job far more happily undertaken in warm, sunny weather than in the doubtful comfort of the workshop in winter. One of the pleasures of working outside is that of occasional pauses to watch a flight of geese going down to the lake, or the swallows which each year nest in the wood store. There is Russell the ram, who always takes an interest in what is going on, and activities over in the pig field and down by the ford offer pleasurable distractions.

We had a little time left in which to clean up a collection of lead-beater's tools, some hay forks, a couple of cleavers and some reaping hooks – all bread and butter stuff or grist to the mill, whichever simile you prefer.

We had a slice of luck in the workshop recently; a pine dresser base from one source exactly matched up with a set of shelves from another. Size and colour were perfect and only small modifications were needed to marry the two. When the job was completed it reminded me of the dresser that stood in the kitchen when I was a boy at home. Perhaps time and distance have dulled my memory of details, but to me it looked just like its twin. Above that dresser there was a row of spring-mounted bells. Six, I think – Front Door, Side Door, Dining Room, Sitting Room, Master Bedroom – perhaps there were only five. In one corner of my little bedroom over the front door there was a loose floorboard. If I lifted the board I could pull the wire which rang the doorbell – a practical joke which was not much appreciated in the kitchen quarters.

Another breed of bells came to hand when William returned from Newark with a mixed bag of purchases, all of them well up to standard. The most strikingly beautiful item was a full set of hand bells, made especially welcome by the fact that they needed no more than a rub over with a duster! They were also good fodder for a series of puns, at which William excels (a facet of life in the workshop on which I have previously elaborated.) 'A good sound purchase', 'sound as a bell', etc.

As often happens when unexpected things turn up, I was reminded of something from the past, in this case my brief encounter with campanology. It is after all one of the great delights of ancient artefacts that they jog the memory and bridge the years.

LOT 24
The King' s Head

Walking down to the post office in the village I met old Jethro. We stood waiting to cross the road by the King's Head watching the traffic fume by; cars, vans and huge bulk transporters piled high with sugar beet. 'Bypass now!' read the poster in the window beside us. We both looked at it and laughed.

'I'll believe it when I see it,' said Jethro, 'they've been on about that bypass for more than twenty years.'

'You must have seen some changes in the village in your time,' I suggested.

'Yiss,' said Jethro, 'What would you say if I told you that more times than I like to remember I've driven as many as a hundred sheep along this road?' There wasn't much I could say, and as we crossed the road he continued: 'I was shepherd in those days at Apple Tree Farm. I used to take them sheep to market along this road, a hundred or more at a time, all on my own 'cept for old Shep, of course. He were a wonderful dog, better than any help I could have had on two legs.'

It being Thursday, we went into the Post Office for our pensions. Happy to hear more, when we came out I suggested stepping into the King's Head for a pint. Jethro took no persuading.

The King's Head, I should mention, is something of a time capsule. The door within the entrance porch opens into a fairly large room. The ceiling is low and there are only two small windows, largely obliterated by the brewer's name in faded gold lettering. At first you see no one in the room. The open fireplace, in which there is usually a good log fire burning, is set around with high-backed settles. (How we would love to get our hands on them. I can visualise them turning a nice profit and hardly touching the ground on their way to America.) The settles form more or less a room within the room, and in the centre is a scrubbed pine table. One of its legs is a little short, or it may be an unevenness in the pamment floor which causes it to rock. Only the uninitiated put their tankards down on it before taking a good pull.

There is no bar and no cellar either. Kegs of beer are set up in a still room at the rear. On the right is a dining room almost filled by another pine table, scoured like driftwood on a beach and surrounded on three sides by wooden benches. The dish of the day is chalked up on a blackboard. I suppose it might be possible to order or even ask diffidently for something else, though I have never heard anyone do so, and it would be foolish as the home-cooked food comes steaming hot and unfailingly delicious. Sometimes the dish of the day is game pie. This never fails to give rise to some sly jokes and a few winks.

Although I find it to be a charming place, Jethro has his reservations. 'You see,' he says, 'there was a time when we had a choice. There were nine pubs in this village. All alike you might say, but oh how different.' (I don't think he knew he was misquoting Wordsworth though I may be wrong, he's deeper than you might think.) 'It's the landlord what makes a pub, either you like him or you doesn't.'

It is rather surprising to think of nine pubs in so small a community, until you remember that there used to be a market here and also, as Jethro pointed out, many more workers lived in the village so that they needed their recreation and entertainment on the spot. 'There weren't no buses into town then. There were at least ten men down on Marsh Farm, the Rookery with at least a dozen horses in the stalls and at least as many men. Church Farm and Hall Farm weren't no different, so the pubs was their clubs and when they hadn't got no money they met at the Forge. That was a great place to get out of the cold in winter and hear all the local gossip, and read the notices stuck on the door – auction sales and elections, things like that.'

On that occasion I didn't learn any more about the life of old style shepherding, but overheard some interesting conversation about ferrets, and I was introduced to Hob Harrison. To begin with, Hob was a reluctant host. He clearly didn't think that I was a suitable person to be taken ferreting. The first thing he made clear was that he didn't want a lot of 'old yapping away' while we were out. All the talk would keep until the day's work was done, and that didn't mean when one got in with the catch. There were important things to be done then such as checking the ferrets for injury or damage and cleaning feet and claws. Apparently it was usual for them to be unharmed, but even rabbits could inflict quite serious damage. 'Then,' he said, 'we'll give them a drink, put them in their cages and you and me'll come back here for a drink and you can talk all you like.'

Which all makes it sound as if I am a great talker and he is a silent type, neither of which is true. It was by sitting very quietly in the corner of the big settle beside the fire in the King's Head that I had been able to listen to all his talk about ferrets and had eventually made my request to be taken on one of his expeditions.

The following Saturday, bright and early, I met Hob at his cottage over the other side of the village. He was already loading his gear into his truck. We went round to the yard where he has his hutches. The ferrets had already been fed, which surprised me, as I had thought it was all part of the act to keep them hungry. Wrong. Next surprise was the quiet gentle way Hob handled them. Crooning softly just as one might attempt to soothe a baby, he stroked and fondled each one as he placed it in his carrying box.

Off we trundled to Warren Hill, stopping several hundred yards short of the warrens and walking quietly over the springy grass. Following instructions I kept a still tongue and watched him as he methodically laid his nets over the mouths of the burrows. When he was satisfied he lifted a jill from her carrying box, stroked her gently and introduced her into one of the burrows.

For several minutes there was complete silence. Then we heard some thumping followed by three almost simultaneous eruptions as three rabbits bolted from the ground and were immediately enmeshed in the purse nets. With a surprising show of speed, Hob reached them one after the other, picked them up by their back legs, still in the nets, and gave each an undoubtedly expert rabbit punch – a karate type chop at the back of the neck.

'I don't like doing that,' said Hob, and later on he detailed other methods of making the kill, none of which will I repeat.

The real surprise to me was that the jill then emerged, seemingly quite content to have enjoyed her brief encounter, and when put back in her box she curled up and had a snooze. This demonstrated the sense in keeping ferrets properly fed.

I was not at all disappointed that we failed to bolt any more rabbits that morning. There were so many questions I wanted to ask and knew that I must wait until we got back to the pub. What I learned then and at later meetings will, I hope, fill a book which I am encouraging Hob to write. It will range beyond ferrets and their legitimate use; the working title is *In vain the net is spread*, but don't hold me to that.

The next day, William and I went to another farm sale. Down the A140, it would have been in the shadow of the Tacolneston television mast only there weren't any shadows; the sky was black with pregnant rainclouds. The large field beside the road would have provided more than adequate parking for the very considerable number of vehicles if it had not been in such a soggy state. Except for one hopeful in an estate car which had to be extracted by a tractor, only 4 x 4s risked it. All the rest of us parked on both sides of the road for about a quarter of a mile. It looked like a sure recipe for disaster.

We pulled on our wellies, put on our funny hats (I think that I must have expounded elsewhere on William's penchant for hats) and plodded with the crowd up the long narrow track to the farm. The house was not a typical Suffolk farmhouse. 'Moated grange' would be a better description. This somehow increased the rude shock of the farm buildings. They immediately brought to mind Stella Gibbons' *Cold Comfort Farm*, so that one was quite prepared to meet 'something nasty in the woodshed'.

The rain now settled into a steady downpour. Even without any further additions, from here on the mud was already liquefied. We ducked (yes, ducks would have been happy) into a decrepit building to view the early lots. There was not much headroom and very little light. No complaints about the quantity of harness, but the state of it all was very sad indeed. Likewise the pathetic collection of hand tools. Three lots of miscellaneous scrap iron could not be faulted. Their miscellaneousness was mind-bending, and one felt that the sheer weight of it all might soon sink into the mud.

There was nothing that William wanted out on the field. Just as well, because it was hard to see how one could have extracted anything from the 'Western Front' quagmire, which was getting worse every minute. We called it a day, washed our boots in a convenient stream beside the track, climbed back into the van and broached our thermos of coffee. 'You can't win every time,' said William, philosophical as usual.

That was not a successful day, but it set me thinking about our wonderful East Coast estuaries. All of them have some points in common. One is the greater or lesser fringe of saltings; delightful aromatic acres of coarse grasses and strange flora and fauna not much found in other habitats, such as samphire, horned poppy, natterjack toads or avocets. The other common factor is mud. At Tollesbury recently, Mary and I walked past the old boat sheds and the new marina, and out along the flood wall towards the Nass. A heron hoisted himself from a drain on the freshwater side and flapped ponderously towards the setting sun. Black-headed gulls were returning from inland towards the estuary.

Out along the bank we sat in the springy grass taking in the beauty of the wide, peaceful panorama. Tide was still on the ebb, exposing broad sheets of glistening mud and countless tiny creeks among tussocks of marsh vegetation. A myriad of trickling rivulets combined in gentle song. Waders hunted busily along the tide line among flotsam of weed and sun-bleached driftwood. Ghostly calls from curlews evoked memories of many anchorages and evening walks on the verges of marshy places.

It is notable that as one goes southward along our coast, the supply of mud becomes increasingly generous. So too does the number of boats of all shapes and sizes. The complexity of those vast fleets of pleasure craft is quite bewildering to one who remembers fleets of small craft and the carefree sailing of the twenties and early thirties.

Marinas have grown up to accommodate the huge increase in numbers. I happen to dislike them – too much like parking lots and multi-storey car parks – but they do offer a practical solution to the problem. They are, perhaps, better than a vast scatter of mud berths with craft crouching like gophers in the mire, spoiling the beauty of the saltings.

Over the years I have had close encounters with East Anglian mud baths, voluntary and otherwise, even up as far as Breydon Water. But then who has not touched the mud there when making passage to or from the

North River? Some of us have touched so firmly that only the next high tide could grant release. I speak of the days of sail when one affected not to know people in motorboats!

The most spectacular mudlarking I recall was a sloppy, slippy, slimy but hilarious experience laying out a mooring at West Mersea. We needed to embed two slabs of concrete as near the fairway as low water would allow. The troop of sea scouts, to which I then belonged, manhandled each load over the mud on an improvised sledge made of corrugated iron. We sank thigh-deep in the mud and were lucky to avoid serious cuts from broken oyster shells.

I have to admit that the sun does not always shine on East Anglia. There are grey days when the sea fret rolls in, when foghorns boom like bitterns in the reed beds, mud and marsh merge, the tide creeps stealthily. Then it is like the second day of the Creation, as the waters move over the firmament and God sees that it is good.

Rugs and carpets – remove curry stains with lemon juice and water.

Stripping – avoid, especially in winter.

Telescopes and timepieces are specialist fields.

Upholstery is a difficult area. Choice of material is personal.

Victoria Cross – rarely on the market. Award medals are valuable. Campaign medals gain with age.

Wood is a magic material which responds to loving care.

LOT 25
Pause for thought

I was sitting in the bathroom cogitating, as one does, when it occurred to me that I know the provenance of every item in the room, except of course the modern fixtures.

The eight-foot-long bamboo towel rail came from a roll of carpet about 50 years ago. It was pressed into service as a tent pole, in which role it served well for several years. Thereafter it was cleaned up and varnished and put to its present use, with a pair of brackets holding it above the radiator.

The Green Man, looking out from the foliage, was an early production of our younger daughter, Fenella, who in those days worked as a potter at Buxton Mill. We have other less pleasing productions around the house, some of which lack easy description and have acquired pet names such as 'the flying corn-plasters' and 'the putrid ostrich egg'. If they lack beauty, they are excellent doorstops.

If you were looking for a typical 1920s medicine cupboard, the one in the corner fills the bill. It has clearly been repainted more than once to conform to the colour scheme in vogue. It is now an unexceptional white as is the floor-to-ceiling cupboard, which has had a more adventurous time. I bought this one in the cattle pens at Diss, and I can't imagine why no one topped my bid of one pound. It was a struggle to get it home and there was no possibility of getting it upstairs. I took it to pieces and rebuilt it *in situ*. A new wooden knob for the door cost almost as much as the cupboard.

One of my favourite memories of those sales is of the time when I bought a proving cupboard; I recognised it from the pages of Mrs Beaton's *Household Management.* A proving cupboard is portable and has no back. It has carrying handles on each side, is usually made of pine, and in its original state is lined with tin. Placed in front of a fire or kitchen range, it can be used for warming plates, dishes and tureens, keeping their contents warm or, as the name implies, for proving bread preparatory to baking. Even now I can remember the excitement of the moment when Lot 99 was offered. In about 30 seconds the cupboard was mine. William and I gave it a full measure of t.l.c. which reaped a just reward.

Back in the bathroom. You don't always expect to find a bookcase. This rather striking oak one has a history; it is reputed to have come from Pakefield Church – that must have been before the church was badly damaged by fire during World War 2. I first saw it in the house of our semi-detached neighbour on Pakefield cliff and later in Notley's saleroom where I bought it. I have been careful to exclude it from the list of fittings and fixtures each time we have moved. A bathroom is not normally a place to find books, but it is a spacious and well ventilated room, built over the old police cell. (That's as good a throwaway line as ever I threw.)

We rather like the wooden wash dolly, which serves as a toilet roll holder. Mary bought it at Evesham. We had some difficulty in removing the words 'washing machine' written on it with a felt-nibbed pen.

The shaving mirror belonged to Mary's grandfather. It is a little beauty – good, thick, bevelled glass one side, and the reverse a magnifying morror of quite frightening strength, very good for lighting a fire in sunshine, but a most unflattering thing first thing in the morning.

There are two rush-seated chairs in the room. As a point of interest, a bathroom is one of the best places for rush-work which does not like dry heat. I must hold myself in check when I get onto the subject of rush-work, as I can go on at great length as it has been one of my favourite occupations.

The smaller of the two chairs came from the refurnished Sunday school at Eastleigh. We bought a number of them and kept that one for old time's sake. The other one is a rare example of a prie-dieu which our elder daughter gave us, and which I re-rushed in 1975 at the Worstead Village Festival. An illustration of this chair appears in William Skull's catalogue of 1852. Rosemary bought it at a splendid emporium near the watermill at Aylsham.

From the sublime to the ridiculous, let me quote from a poem by Mabel Lucy Atwell, which hung on the wall in the bathroom when I was a small boy, living in Norwich.

> 'Please remember, don't forget,
> Never leave the bathroom wet,
> Nor leave the soap still in the water;
> That's a thing you never oughter,
> Nor keep the bath an hour or more
> When other folks are wanting one,
> Just don't forget, it isn't done.
> And if you rally do the thing,
> There's not the slightest need to sing.'

And I note that Mabel Lucy Atwell memorabilia is now fetching very good prices.

LOT 26
A good finish

Quite often in a sale catalogue the last few numbers are left open in case some late items need to be included. We have now reached that point.

You might think I was spinning a yarn if I told you that William and I once restored three spinning wheels in a morning. It's strange how this sort of thing happens. One might not set eyes on one for a period of years, and then three converge on the scene all at once. One of them didn't belong to William, it had been brought in by another dealer for t.l.c., and as you might expect, that one needed a good deal more attention than the two which he had bought.

One would hardly imagine that attaching the three legs to each base-board could be anything but simple. Complications arose from the fact that the board, when in its final position, is not horizontal, and with half a dozen holes to choose from there are several possible permutations. Sorting out that little problem was reminiscent of the old music-hall turn of the man with a folding deck-chair, and it doesn't take a lot to get us laughing.

To be honest, a spinning wheel is not a complicated piece of machinery, though it does look a bit of a mystery when all the components are jumbled together in a dirty cardboard box, together with sundry other items which have nothing to do with it. Assembly was a nice mixture of simple engineering and furniture restoration. We cleaned and polished everything for a start. The maidens and mothers-of-all responded especially well, being, I suspect, impregnated with lanolin. The only significant damage was in the relatively fragile fliers (or spindle-whorls, as some call them.)

Although it is highly unlikely that any one of these three will ever be used for spinning, professional pride demanded that we got the mechanisms working properly. Even if displayed solely as decorative objects, few people will be able to resist having a go with the treadles. There are, of course, a number of hand-weavers to be found – try Worstead Church if you are interested. It could be called a universal craft. Every country has its own type of apparatus for spinning and weaving, all of them basically similar, but I suspect that only the most dedicated hand-weavers will be spinning their own yarns. It used to be said that it took eight hand-spinners to keep one hand-weaver supplied.

As recently as 1932 (well, actually, that doesn't sound very recent, I was twelve years old at that date), spinning wheels were still in use in Northern Scotland for the manufacture of worsted yarns. Thank God for Mr Arkwright, one might say, and then reflect sadly that today, even in

Manchester, one would probably listen in vain for the racket of even a single Spinning Jenny.

With a final flourish we fixed the cords connecting the treadles to the cranks on the wheels (the more decorative model had a wooden footman instead of a cord.) Inevitably, William had a go at treadling. The wooden treadle went thump, thump, on the floor.

'We'd better shorten that cord,' said William, 'The people downstairs won't like that.'

I thought of the spinning wheels this morning because today we are involved with the very beginning of the process – it's sheep-shearing time again. D.I.Y. has grabbed us in many forms, but sheep-shearing is no longer one of them. William did have a go at it one year but the result was not pretty. When Reg comes and does the job with amazing speed and dexterity, the ewes look as if they have taken on a new lease of life. Russell the Ram emerges less fortunate. For one thing he definitely suffers from a great loss of stature and dignity, as his fleece is magnificent and makes him look twice as large as life. The other factor is the gross scar on his back which again becomes visible. Poor chap, he had a severe agricultural accident in his youth and will always carry the mark. He took a dislike to his hay rack this morning and demolished it, though normally he is quite placid and answers when spoken to. I don't think that he can actually manage a smile; he is more like one of Mary's Dalmatians which she said could smile, but I thought it looked more like a leer or even the beginnings of a snarl.

However, this is clearly 'look back and smile' time. Some of the most charming smiles which I remember belonged to the American servicemen's wives who were good customers at the Old Forge, and some of them became good friends. Who could forget Celeste and the time she walked into the forge, saw the curved-back settle, stamped her foot and said, 'I gotta have that...'? Later she sent us a photograph from the States showing the settle established in their ranch-house.

On one occasion we set up our stall by invitation at the Officers' Wives' Charity Bazaar. The huge aircraft hangar in which the event was staged made Norwich Cathedral look like a small parish church. There was plenty of brisk business transacted and we were happy to be a part of it. The scent of barbecued spareribs wafted in from the tarmac outside. For two days we lived on such delicacies as spring rolls, popcorn, burgers and an endless supply of coffee served by our charming hostesses. It was a little piece of America set down in East Anglia.

It is well known that customers can be most tiresome people with awkward habits, strange ideas about credit and not noticeably good manners. In this field, as in others, our experiences were much happier than we ever thought possible, not only pleasant but in many cases downright enjoyable, with numbers developing into good friends. I remember one refugee from the Home Counties who said, 'You don't sound as if you come from round here.'

'Perhaps,' I replied, 'that is because I went to school in Surrey.' It transpired that she lived in College Road, Epsom, only a few yards from the school gates.

In similar vein I was asked, 'Do you find that the locals accept you?' At that date, with sixty-eight years in East Anglia behind me, I rather thought of myself as a local.

Once one starts looking back (and I note that I was doing that right at the beginning of this book) the memories come flooding in, falling over each other. In our time Mary and I have attended a variety of evening classes – colloquial French, Geology of East Anglia, Rush-work, Upholstery, Cookery (billed as 'French Cookery Without Garlic'!) and Flower Arranging among them. William's excursions into further education started more formally with a degree course in Estate Management at Reading University, followed by a green period of self-sufficiency with a sideline in furniture removals, employments with an estate agent, Norwich City Council and a spell in a reproduction furniture factory. All grist to the mill, or as Mary's grandmother liked to say, 'You can always learn something from the biggest old fool'.

My rush-work proved to be a useful accomplishment. I had attended classes long before we became involved in the antiques business, and was able to put it to good use. At one stage while we were at the Old Forge most of my rush-work was going to America. Sometimes my pleasure was touched with sadness as I watched the results of my labours being loaded up for the first stage of the journey to Chicago. The last one I saw go was a high-backed rocking chair, a beautiful piece of furniture. The honey hues of ash and elm and the mellow tones of Norfolk rushes glowed in the sunshine as the chair was carried into the cavernous interior of the pantechnicon.

On an entirely different subject, I recall listening to William bargaining with a father and son plumbing partnership. The son was saying, 'We heard this old pub isn't a pub no more and we remembered them urinals. Pale blue, and with all their copperwork polished up they looked real picturesque. Just what we need for a job over at Dickleburgh.' A bargain was struck, with both parties well satisfied. I think of that occasion as a good example of the expression 'A good deal'.

Another interesting bargain which William struck at the Swan was with Reuben, the itinerant fibrous plasterer: board and lodging, plus a small sum of money in exchange for the design and execution of an area of pargeting on the gable-end of the building. We soon learned that plastering is very thirsty work. Plaster and plasterer dried out very quickly.

An early experience I had in bargaining at the Old Forge left me feeling rather limp but with one thousand pounds in my hand, the first and I believe the last time such a thing ever happened to me. It was fascinating seeing the notes peeled off a wad from a back pocket.

One can laugh with something near disbelief when thinking of some of the strange bygones that we bought and which other people were strange enough to buy from us. A well-sinker's windlass, blacksmith's bellows, a tin bath shaped like a boot, potato-pickers' baskets, cartwheels, fire buckets and the Duke of Grafton's egg rack, to name only a few. Then, just when you think you have seen everything, you do a couple of house clearances and find something ridiculous like a left-handed corkscrew or an ostrich egg engraved 'Inkermann 1854' or those two motorbikes in a bedroom – which accounted for the dark oily stain on the ceiling of the room below. The stain had looked so much like blood that we were quite fearful of going upstairs. A house clearance rarely fails to produce something out of the ordinary.

I have only recently been introduced to the mega antiques fairs, the ones which are staged at places such as Newark, Swinderbury, and, more recently, at Oakington. William buys and sells at these events, and took me to see what it was all about. They are, in effect, your local car boot sale expanded almost beyond belief. They usually take place on disused airfields, the rows of marquees and stalls forming a small village. As they are normally two-day affairs, facilities for stallholders are provided in the form of portaloos, washrooms and shower units and some on-site catering. There are dealers and merchandise from as far afield as Central Europe – a polyglot gallimaufry. Convincing repro high-backed Windsor chairs may be flanked by a deep-sea diver's suit and a stuffed dog; beautiful garden furniture will be offset by equally hideous garden furniture. You will find superb pine furniture, some genuine antiques, jewellery, china, glassware, everything that you have ever thought of, and much that you would never have thought of in a month of Sundays.

As William and I walked round, John called on his mobile to find out our whereabouts; if he had turned round he would have seen us. We adjourned to a coffee stall and compared notes. Antique oak furniture is his speciality, though like any good dealer he doesn't wear blinkers. I couldn't say how far we walked that day; it was a moderately tiring exercise. Back at the well-organised car park we picked up the car and drove gently round the stalls where William had struck bargains, loaded the roof rack and drove to Cambridge.

At 'Those were the Days' in Mill Road we carried in some new stock and rearranged William's exhibition in the basement, making a superb fitted carpenter's chest the focal point. After we left, the management were so taken by the chest that they brought it up from the basement and incorporated it into the window display. It sold within the week. I was not surprised; it had such a delicious patina. 'Patina' is defined in my dictionary as 'a sheen acquired from constant handling or contact', alternatively 'a film or surface resulting from long exposure or burial'!

How often have we heard John Blyth say, 'What wonderful patina,' as he caresses the surface of some cherished piece of furniture? Arthur Negus was just the same, always enthusiastic about the subject, and stroking the wood with that characteristic sweep of his hand, clearly enjoying the visual and tactile pleasure.

Several years ago we began to think that the popularity of pine furniture was beginning to wane. We were wrong. What had begun to decline was the supply of good quality old pine furniture. Reproduction and modern pine began to take off, and continued to fly high. This is good news for conservationists, as softwood forests are relatively quickly renewable resources. Good news for us too, as, although we are happy to work on hardwoods and exotics, pine has always been our bread and butter, and without any modesty I claim that we have reached a fair degree of expertise.

Of course it is not possible to achieve true patina on most restored furniture, but it is possible to go a long way towards it with patience and hard work. When, as is so often, it is necessary to rub down pine to recreate that sought-after finish, mechanical aids help to get there, but in the end there is no substitute for hard work, fine grade glass-paper and steel wool.

With a smooth sheen achieved, which is such a pleasure to stroke, there are then a number of options, the choice of which depends on personal taste, or on a specific customer's requirement, or it may be dictated by the eventual use to which the article will be put.

'We've got an odd one here,' said William the other day. 'The customer wants thick cork linoleum laid on these two tables. I think it is something to do with electronic equipment.'

Even now we still find ourselves taking on new, strange tasks for the first time. Getting the lino took some time, and then we waited for the manufacturer's advice on the best adhesive to use, so the weeks went by before we could start working on the job. Then it was straightforward, and we even had some splines in stock of exactly the right thickness to use as edgings. The job was certainly easier than the routine task of rubbing down those tabletops, removing stains, filling and wax polishing.

The range of wax polishes available has grown enormously. In our early days we used ordinary domestic polish for general use and an expensive petroleum-based wax for highlighting furniture, with special regard for those portions along which our clients customarily ran their fingers! Now William has a shelf entirely devoted to wax polishes for a range of colours and other special uses. We have always had one or two tins of stain available for touching up. An odd feature we have noticed is that nine times out of ten American walnut gives the desired result.

Painting is a rare event except on metalwork such as garden furniture, and that itself is a seasonal feature. It is not very sensible trying to sell garden furniture in December, when firedogs, companion sets and log

baskets are more in vogue. In fact, the only furniture I can remember painting has been an occasional lick of green inside corner cupboards.

Mary was always regarded as our metal polishing expert. I should perhaps say cleaner, as there is often a fair amount of cleaning to be done before reaching the polishing stage. My thoughts turned today to all Mary's energetic polishing as I watched William at work with the buffing wheel - yet another mechanical aid producing pristine results with greatly reduced physical effort when operated with skill.

Mentioning those fireside accoutrements reminds me of the time I took a brass-handled poker to a blacksmith for repair. It was some years ago in North Norfolk. I called a couple of times before it was ready. He had done a beautiful job, and when I asked how much I owed him he said 'Half a crown.'

'Come on,' I said, 'there's no such thing as half a crown now.'

'Oh blast, no,' he said, 'I'd better say two bob.'

Well, I'm still resentful though more or less resigned to decimal coinage, but I shall always measure in feet and inches.

My final offering is a quotation from one of William's suppliers' catalogue and price lists:

'Coffin varnish for a fine finish'.